VCDX Boot Camp

Preparing for the
VCDX Panel Defense

VMware Press is the official publisher of VMware books and training materials, which provide guidance on the critical topics facing today's technology professionals and students. Enterprises, as well as small- and medium-sized organizations, adopt virtualization as a more agile way of scaling IT to meet business needs. VMware Press provides proven, technically accurate information to help them meet their goals for customizing, building, and maintaining their virtual environment.

With books, certification and study guides, video training, and learning tools produced by world-class architects and IT experts, VMware Press helps IT professionals master a diverse range of topics on virtualization and cloud computing. It is the official source of reference materials for preparing for the VMware Certified Professional Examination.

VMware Press is also pleased to have localization partners that can publish its products in more than forty-two languages, including, but not limited to, Chinese (Simplified), Chinese (Traditional), French, German, Greek, Hindi, Japanese, Korean, Polish, Russian, and Spanish.

For more information about VMware Press, please visit **vmwarepress.com**.

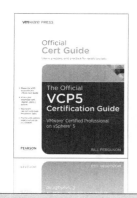

VCDX Boot Camp

Preparing for the
VCDX Panel Defense

John Yani Arrasjid, Ben Lin, Mostafa Khalil

vmware® PRESS

Upper Saddle River, NJ • Boston • Indianapolis • San Francisco
New York • Toronto • Montreal • London • Munich • Paris • Madrid
Capetown • Sydney • Tokyo • Singapore • Mexico City

VCDX Boot Camp: Preparing for the VCDX Panel Defense

Warning and Disclaimer

Corporate and Government Sales

VMware Press offers excellent discounts on this book when ordered in quantity for bulk purchases or special sales, which may include electronic versions and/or custom covers and content particular to your business, training goals, marketing focus, and branding interests. For more information, please contact:

U.S. Corporate and Government Sales
(800) 382-3419
corpsales@pearsontechgroup.com

For sales outside the United States, please contact:

International Sales
international@pearsoned.com

Library of Congress Control Number: 2013904949

Text printed in the United States on recycled paper at RR Donnelley in Crawfordsville, Indiana

First Printing April 2013

VMWARE PRESS BUSINESS OWNERS
Erik Ullanderson
Anand Sundaram

ASSOCIATE PUBLISHER
David Dusthimer

ACQUISITIONS EDITOR
Joan Murray

DEVELOPMENT EDITOR
Marianne Bartow

TECHNICAL EDITORS
Doug Baer
Michael Webster

MANAGING EDITOR
Sandra Schroeder

PROJECT EDITOR
Mandie Frank

COPY EDITOR
Krista Hansing Editorial Services

PROOFREADER
Gill Editorial Services

DESIGNER
Chuti Prasertsith

COMPOSITOR
Bumpy Design

EDITORIAL ASSISTANT
Vanessa Evans

To Amy, Catherine, Sofi, Lila, Mom, and Dad, who have supported all my projects and helped put a balance between life and work. I love you.
— John Yani Arrasjid

To Mom and Dad
— Ben Lin

To my wife and best friend, Gloria, for her unconditional love
— Mostafa Khalil

Contents

Foreword   xiii

Introduction   xvii

About the Authors   xxi

About the Reviewers   xxiii

Acknowledgments   xxv

Chapter 1   Certification Overview   1

   VMware Certification Program Framework   3

   Certification Tracks   5

      VCDX for Datacenter Virtualization (VCDX-DCV)   7

      VCDX for Desktop (VCDX-DT)   7

      VCDX for Cloud (VCDX-Cloud)   8

      The VCDX Process   9

      Value Proposition   10

   Review   11

Chapter 2   Preparation   13

   Experience   14

      What Demonstrates Design Expertise?   14

      What Demonstrates a Lack of Design Experience?   15

   The Application   16

      Application Submission Process   17

      VCDX Application   18

   Creating a VCDX Study Group   21

   Practice and Supporting Materials   21

   VCDX Panelist Restrictions   21

   Running a VCDX Panel Defense Boot Camp   22

   Practice   22

   Room Layout   23

   Running the Defense Within a Set Timeline   24

   Mock Defense Checklist   25

   Review   25

Chapter 3   The Design   27

Assembling Your Design   28

    VCDX Design Defense Blueprint   28

    Method   32

    Traceability   33

    Resolving Conflicts   34

    Sizes Matters Not   35

    Design Artifacts   36

    What Makes for a Good Design?   36

    Conceptual Model   36

    Logical Design   38

    Physical Design   39

    Justification   39

    Impact   39

    Localization   39

    Checklist: Design Selection and Content   40

Summary   40

Chapter 4   Defense Overview   43

The Interview Process   43

Before the Defense   44

Time Management   44

Panel Defense Participants   45

Environment   46

Panelists' Perspective   46

    Sitting in the Panelist Seat   46

    Panelist Qualifications   47

    Panelist Preparation   47

    Panelist Expectations   47

Notification of Results   47

Chapter 5   Design Defense   49

Design Overview Presentation   50

    Example Presentation Slides   51

    Reference Material   53

Know Your Design   54

Defense Strategy   54

    Practice Leads to Success   55

    Preparation Checklists   56

Review   58

Chapter 6   The Design Scenario   59

Showcase Your Skills   59

Panelist's Perspective   61

Design Scenario Examples   62

    Design Scenario 1   62

    Design Scenario 2   66

    Design Scenario 3   70

    The Art of Explanations   73

    Design Scenario 4   77

Review   78

Chapter 7   The Troubleshooting Scenario   81

Conducting the Troubleshooting Scenario   81

Thinking Aloud   82

Asking Questions   82

Using a Whiteboard or Paper   82

Troubleshooting Analysis   82

    Example: Conflicting Information   83

    Requirements Analysis   83

    The Panelist Perspective   83

Example Scenarios   83

    Example Troubleshooting Scenario #1   84

    Example Troubleshooting Scenario #2   89

    Example Troubleshooting Scenario #3   93

    Example Troubleshooting Scenario #4   98

Review   102

Conclusion   103

References   105

Books and Links   105

Training Courses   106

Glossary   107

Index   111

Foreword

In my role as VMware's Chief Technology Officer for more than 11 years, I see education as important throughout one's life, especially in advancing one's career. I had the pleasure of attending Stanford University in the early 1990s. There, I met the founders of VMware and worked on a project that would become the foundation of our company. This education-centric environment was the perfect petri dish for the growth of this amazing company. Such environments require you to step back and gain perspective before jumping into something new. They also provide a burst of can-do spirit that helps you take on problems that might otherwise be far too daunting. This combination of education and confidence helped launch our company. That same great combination is present in the VMware Certified Design Expert (VCDX) program.

I'd like to welcome you to this enablement tool that teaches the VMware Architecture Design principles and methods embodied in the VCDX program. These same principals and methods were used in developing the industry-recognized vCloud Architecture Toolkit (vCAT) to enable architects, administrators, and consumers of Cloud to realize the full potential of this revolutionary technology. For this reason, VCDX holders are considered a hot commodity; they are recognized as thought leaders in a dynamic industry with almost unlimited growth potential. Joining this elite group is a journey that does not end with achieving the certification. It requires continuous education, the ability to learn from your experiences, and a structured approach to addressing customer needs in your designs. It is not easy to become a VCDX, but it is certainly easier if you have a mentor—or, better yet, three—to help you begin the journey.

Having worked with John and Mostafa for more than 10 years, I trust that their guidance will absolutely meet your high expectations. I've been watching John play in Elastic Sky, VMware's house band, since 2004, including when the band opened for Foreigner, INXS, the Killers, and John Bon Jovi. Mostafa I've also known for a long time: He was one of our very early employees and is an industry-recognized storage expert in virtualization; his signature is on an I-beam in our corporate Promontory building complex. Ben continues to actively work on cloud solutions as a Cloud Specialist. I have supported the work that he, John, and Mostafa have done both inside and outside VMware.

John started development work on the VCDX Boot Camp back in 2008. At the same time, he started the VCDX tips series on Twitter, which thousands of aspiring virtualization architects follow. The VCDX boot camps and the VCDX tips were so successful that readers asked for a compendium of these tips, to help peel back the curtain of mystery that seems to surround the certification. In this book, John, Ben, and Mostafa have worked to cover the important details that can help you successfully develop designs as you work toward the ultimate goal of achieving VCDX.

The VMware Certification Program began early in the history of VMware, when x86 virtualization was revolutionary and the program focused on our original Workstation, GSX, and ESX products. Because the technology was new, there was a requirement to educate end users and practitioners and to validate expertise to employers and customers. Since that time, VMware has continued to grow and innovate. The company has revolutionized End User Computing and introduced the world to Cloud and the Software-Defined Data Center. The certification program has evolved and now includes the Professional (VCP), Advanced Professional (VCAP), and Expert (VCDX) levels, each with several areas of specialization.

VCDX now covers data center virtualization with VCDX-DCV, desktop with VCDX-DT, and cloud computing with VCDX-Cloud. This supports the specialized architecture design skills required to serve the growing needs of our customers (internal, external, big business, small business), partners, and internal teams.

The team has provided a history of the program, best practices and tips for success, and actual scenarios that you can use in running your own boot camps, study sessions, or mock defenses. In your daily work life, you can reference this book to help you take a VCDX-style approach for design success. This book will help you understand this highly sought-after certification with supporting material to help improve your scoring potential. It provides details that remove some of the mysteries and mystique behind the program, including the in-person design defense. If you are a VCP- or VCAP-certified individual, you can learn more about the practices VCDX holders use in developing robust, complex, computing environments with VMware and related technologies.

The VCDX program is now in its sixth year. It differentiates individuals by requiring them to prove certain skills in front of a panel of VCDX, in much the same way a Master's or PhD defense is done. The process demands significant time and effort, but everyone can benefit from going through it. As I've said to VMware employees, the VCDX is VMware's PhD equivalent.

I believe that success in developing technology, services, and solutions and using these in customer solutions requires a solid base of expert-level architecture skills, with VCDX at the top. The benefits to an architect might appear obvious, but others who learn the VCDX design method also reap benefits. This can include understanding how to review designs others have created.

It's been an amazing ride at VMware for so many reasons, including the great products, legendary customer success stories, and a whole new partner ecosystem around virtualization. But the reason I've enjoyed the ride the most has been my fellow employees and their amazing work. You'll be hard-pressed to find anyone who exemplifies the VMware spirit like John, Mostafa, and Ben. Guys, congratulations on a great book, and I'll be looking forward to seeing you in action again at VMworld. And to all the readers, I wish you the best on your journey as an architect!

Dr. Stephen Herrod, PhD
General Catalyst, Managing Director
March 2013

Introduction

A journey of a thousand miles begins with a single step.

—Lao-Tzu

Attaining VMware Certified Design Expert (VCDX) certification can seem like a daunting proposition. Numerous exams are required. Hour are consumed preparing a comprehensive application package. The final step is an oral interview that has unnerved even the most experienced architects.

Anyone with the desire to improve and develop certain skills is well on the path toward VCDX. The amount of time invested in the process varies based on your current experience and skills. The journey may seem long and arduous, but it is because this accreditation represents the pinnacle of VMware certification. That alone provides much of the incentive and allure.

Initially, the clandestine nature of the process enhanced the appeal. This wasn't intentional—just a by-product of a radically new advanced certification. The void was partially filled by bloggers, followed by a proactive approach towards eliminating confusion through increased transparency. This book further demystifies the process and provides a systematic approach.

Embarking on the path yields benefits even if the end result does not include attainment of expert certification. The path is time consuming and challenging, but the entire process is a tremendous learning experience. For many people, achieving the highest certification is the starting point, not the culmination, of a longer journey toward mastering technology architecture and greater things to come.

The points made in this book are common, and you may have already considered them to some degree. The intent is not to provide cookie-cutter instruction manuals, which only stifle creativity. Instead, we share insight and perspective based on prior experiences, to structure and guide your approach. That said, reading a book on architecture does not make one an architect. There is no substitute for real-world experience.

Years of design experience and mastery of enterprise architecture are not needed to make the attempt. It's largely about gaining experience—the *right* experience—and learning from those who have come before you. This book aims to put you on the right trajectory.

Will you take on the challenge? Your journey begins now.

Who Should Read This Book

VCDX certification is for virtualization architects and has demonstrated a large value proposition. With the expansion, we now have certifications covering data center virtualization (VCDX-DCV), cloud (VCDX-Cloud), and desktop (VCDX-DT) technologies. If you are currently working with VMware technologies and solutions as an architect, any one of these could be a valuable certification for you. This book helps peel back the curtain and removes the mystery behind both the VCDX program and the recommendations for success in the Panel Defense.

Goals and Methods

The primary goal of this book is to increase the number of VCDX individuals supporting VMware solutions.

To aid you in gaining the knowledge and understanding of success criteria, this book includes the following components:

- **Prerequisites:** This component defines what is needed to reach the Panel Defense. It includes the prerequisites and the recommended steps for completing them. It also provides suggestions on selecting and developing a design and completing the application process.

- **The Defense:** This component describes what is included in the defense, the timelines, and selected methods for preparation. It covers all three areas of defending your design and conducting the design and troubleshooting scenarios.

- **The Design Scenario:** Chapter 6 "The Design Scenario," includes recommendations for conducting the design scenario. It provides four sample design scenarios, with analysis, to help you understand what is expected of a candidate in architecting a solution.

- **The Troubleshooting Scenario:** Chapter 7 "The Troubleshooting Scenario," includes recommendations for conducting the troubleshooting scenario. It provides four design scenarios, with analysis, to help you understand the skills and approach required of a candidate in troubleshooting a problem from an architect perspective.

How to Use This Book

This book was written in the order that the authors believe is best for learning about the program, preparing for the defense, and conducting the defense. If you are familiar with the VCDX program, you can skip to select chapters as needed. If you are new to the program, we recommend that you read the book cover to cover. This book enables you to target specific areas to which you want to devote additional time or attention. It provides the flexibility to move among chapters as you work on the different areas on which candidates are evaluated. The sections are also designed to support you in conducting a mock defense, a boot camp, or a study session with others.

The core chapters, Chapters 1 through 7, cover the following topics:

- **Chapter 1, "Certification Overview."** This chapter focuses on the certification program and the history behind the development of the VCDX program.

- **Chapter 2, "Preparation."** This chapter focuses on the required steps in preparing for your defense. It also provides recommendations for running your own boot camp or study group.

- **Chapter 3, "The Design."** This chapter focuses on selecting and creating a design, embellishing the content with design decisions and design patterns to support the VCDX Blueprint. It helps you understand all aspects within the design and other supporting documents.

- **Chapter 4, "Defense Overview."** This chapter focuses on what is involved in the panel defense. It provides a recommended approach for each of the three parts of the defense.

- **Chapter 5, "Design Defense."** This chapter focuses on the details in the first part of the defense. It includes tips for developing your presentation and responding to panelist questions.

- **Chapter 6, "The Design Scenario."** This chapter focuses on the progression of the design scenario. It provides details on how to work through the session for this section and achieve maximum scoring opportunities. The chapter includes four example design scenarios, covering VCDX-DCV, VCDX-Cloud, and VCDX-DT.

- **Chapter 7, "The Troubleshooting Scenario."** This chapter focuses on the progression of the troubleshooting scenario. It provides details on how to work through the session provided for this section and achieve maximum scoring opportunities. The chapter includes four example troubleshooting scenarios, covering VCDX-DCV, VCDX-Cloud, and VCDX-DT.

Preparation is essential—do not rush the process. Allocate sufficient time to complete and submit a solid design that meets the VCDX Blueprint guidelines. For defense schedules and additional program details, check out the VMware Certified Design Expert site at http://www.vmware.com/go/vcdx.

The VCDX Panel Defense and This Book

The material included in this book comes from five years of conducting panel defenses. This book includes additional quotes and insights from other VCDXs who wanted to share their unique experience.

Book Content Updates and Bonus Material

VMware Press will periodically post additional content on the web page associated with this book, at http://www.pearsonitcertification.com/title/9780321910592. We also recommend that you periodically check this page on the Pearson IT Certification website to view any errata or supporting book files that are available.

About the Authors

 **John Y. Arrasjid, VCDX-001**, is a Principal Architect at VMware, leading development of VMware Validated Architectures. He has been with VMware since 2003. He developed IP and software for his first six years as a Consulting Architect and currently does so as a Principal Architect, VMware Ambassador, and vExpert. John regularly speaks at VMware conferences and related workshops and industry events, including VMworld, VMware Partner Exchange, VMware vForum, VMware User Groups (VMUG), and the USENIX LISA conference.

John has been the lead architect and chief product owner for the VMware vCloud Architecture Toolkit (vCAT) since 2011. The latest release of vCAT 3.1 will be released through VMware Press in printed format; the online electronic version is accessible for free at http://www.vmware.com/go/vcat.

John's publications include three books in the USENIX Association Short Topics in System Administration series: *Deploying the VMware Infrastructure*, *Foundation for Cloud Computing with VMware vSphere 4*, and *Cloud Computing with VMware vCloud Director*.

During his past ten years at VMware, John has developed multiple consulting engagement materials and conference tutorials that focus on security, performance, and availability of virtualized and cloud infrastructures. John's earlier work at VMware included development of free backup (vmsnap) and recovery (vmres) tools for VMs using snapshot technology.

John participated in the initial development of the VCDX program and continues his support with online and onsite workshops (VCDX Tips, VCDX Boot Camp, #vBrownbag Boot Camp Live Online) and this book.

John is a member of the USENIX Association (and LISA SIG), where he serves as vice president of the Board of Directors. He can be followed on Twitter as @vcdx001 and can be seen playing guitar and ukulele with the VMware Elastic Sky band and at The Strawberry Music Festival.

Ben Lin, VCDX-045, is currently a Global Cloud Specialist and has been with VMware since 2008. He holds VCDX3/4/5 certifications and actively participates in VCDX panels and development activities. Ben graduated from the University of California, Berkeley with a Bachelor of Science in Electrical Engineering and Computer Sciences.

Ben coauthored the book *Cloud Computing with VMware vCloud Director* and was closely involved with cloud designs and deployments since the inception of vCloud Director. He works with global customers in the Americas, providing thought leadership and expertise in designing cloud solutions.

Ben has been a lead architect for the VMware vCloud Architecture Toolkit (vCAT) and has created numerous reference architectures, service kits, and whitepapers used by field and partners worldwide. He regularly presents at conferences such as VMworld, VMworld Europe, Partner Exchange, LISA, HotCloud, and vForum. Follow him on Twitter at @blin23.

Mostafa Khalil, VCDX-002, is a Technical Support Director on the Global Support Services team. He has been with VMware since 1999, at the top of the escalation ladder in support.

Mostafa specializes in storage-related technologies and holds VCDX3/4/5 certifications. He has published the book *Storage Implementation in vSphere 5.0, Technology Deep Dive.*

Mostafa regularly speaks at VMware conferences and workshops (VMworld and Partner Exchange) and other industry events. Follow him on Twitter at @mostafaVMW.

About the Reviewers

Doug Baer, VCDX-019 (@dobaer), is an Infrastructure Architect on the Hands-on Labs team in VMware's Technical Marketing group. He works on the infrastructure used to deliver content for VMworld conferences, online labs (http://hol.vmware.com), and events throughout the year.

Doug's 19 years in IT span a variety of roles and industries. His job responsibilities have included design, implementation, and operation of directory services, network and storage infrastructure solutions, training and lab management, and system administration. Doug has a Bachelor of Science in Computer Science from the University of Arizona and holds several top-level industry certifications, including VMware Certified Design Expert (VCDX) and HP's Master ASE Converged Infrastructure Architect. He has been a session presenter and content contributor to the hands-on labs at VMworld conferences and regularly serves on the review board for certifying new Master ASE-CI candidates.

Michael Webster, VCDX-066 (@vcdxnz001), based in Auckland, New Zealand, is a VMware Certified Design Expert on vSphere 4 and 5 and vExpert 2012. He is the owner of IT Solutions 2000 Ltd. (founded in 2000), which delivers project management, ITIL-based VMware operational readiness, and technical architecture consulting services to government, enterprise, and service provider clients around the world.

Michael has been designing and deploying VMware solutions since 2002 as a consultant or project manager. He specializes in the design and project implementation of virtualization solutions for UNIX-to-Linux migrations, business-critical applications, disaster avoidance, mergers and acquisitions, and public and private cloud. Michael has been in the IT industry since 1995 and has consulted as a project manager and architect since 2001. He is regularly called on to consult and speak on all aspects of virtualizing business-critical applications at events and for organizations across the globe. Michael also holds VCP-DT, VCP-Cloud, MCSE (NT-2003), and ITIL Foundation, and he is experienced in PMP and Prince 2 project-management methodologies. He is an avid supporter of the VMware community and is the author and maintainer of the Long White Virtual Clouds blog (http://longwhiteclouds.com), which discusses all things related to VMware, cloud, and virtualizing business-critical applications.

Acknowledgments

The authors would like to thank the following people for their support in developing and reviewing the material included. Thank you to our family and friends who supported our efforts in creating this work.

Thank you to the VMware Press team and the certification team, including Erik Ullanderson, Mark Brunstad, Jill Liles, Lisa Leong, and Melissa Tuite. Thank you to our team at Pearson Technology Group, including Joan Murray (editor) and David Dusthimer (associate publisher). Thank you to Marianne Bartow (development editor) and Mandie Frank (project editor).

Thank you to Duncan Epping (VCDX-007), Wade Holmes (VCDX-015), Yvo Wiskere (VCDX-025), Frank Denneman (VCDX-029), and Chris Colotti (VCX-037) for providing quotes and historical perspective.

Thank you to our deep-dive technical reviewers Michael Webster (VCDX-066) and Doug Baer (VCDX-019).

A special thank you for detailed review input goes to Duncan Epping (VCDX-007) and Aidan Dalgleish (VCDX-010).

Thank you also to additional reviewers who provided generous feedback: Craig Risinger (VCDX-006), Mohan Potheri (VCDX-098), Phil Callahan (candidate), Jill Liles (VCDX Marketing Manager), and Cody Bunch (candidate).

Thank you to our past and present VMware management team especially Peter Giordano, Michael "Dino" Cicciarelli, Stephen Beck, Raj Ramanujam, Matthew Stepanski, Scott Bajtos, Marty Messer, Pat Gelsinger, and Todd Ulrich.

It takes a large team to do this, and others have provided contributions besides those listed here. We thank them also.

John, Ben, Mostafa

Chapter 1

Certification Overview

An investment in knowledge pays the best interest.

—Benjamin Franklin

Certification is a strategic weapon for companies, offering technologists the opportunity to achieve higher distinction and marketability while also building a community of identifiable experts. The growth and adoption of virtualization provided the impetus to extend beyond the well-known VMware Certified Professional (VCP) certification. Development of the VMware Certified Design Expert (VCDX) program began in 2007, driven by market demand to recognize differentiated skill sets for administrators and architects.

With marching orders to create an exam befitting the most senior VMware architects, the certification team collaborated with a group of VMware Professional Services (PSO) architects to define and scope the eventual program. The assembled team included individuals with a diverse set of architecture design skills. The goal was to identify the skill sets necessary in designing, implementing, and operating a VMware-based virtual infrastructure. The development team included Melissa Tuite, John Arrasjid, Mostafa Khalil, Kamau Wanguhu, Andrew Hald, Mahesh Rajani, Craig Risinger, Duncan Epping, Richard Damoser, Ryan Baker, Russ Henmi, Shridhar Deuskar, and several others. Mark Brunstad currently handles program stewardship, a title previously held by Christen Patterson, Brian Rice, and Melissa Tuite.

To ensure the legal defensibility of the certification, the team gathered in Palo Alto, California, where they received training on psychometric analysis and testing methodology. Psychometrics analysis deals with measuring a candidate through testing and assessments.

Ease of localization was also a priority when constructing the question pool, to accelerate broader uptake worldwide.

Candidate validation includes confirming design-level skills during the VCAP Datacenter Design (VCAP-DCD) certification exam. A freeform graphical tool was needed to provide a mechanism for validating design skills in a testing center. Developers created a tool that allowed placement and linkage of multiple objects. Craig Risinger worked to develop the initial test questions to validate a candidate on their design skills.

Certification development requires careful coordination and collaboration across multiple teams. One of the most time-consuming aspects is developing the design and trouble-shooting scenarios that represent a realistic environment based on similar situations experienced by VMware customers and partners. Scenario details are covered in Chapter 6, "The Design Scenario," and Chapter 7, "The Troubleshooting Scenario."

If a panel consists of three VCDXs, how were the first few certified if no panelists existed at the time? It's the classic "chicken or egg" causality dilemma. With live defense requirements, non-VCDX panel members certified the first set of architects to bootstrap the program. The initial panelists invariably achieved certification under the same constraints and guidelines. Each member of the original team had seven panelists to validate and refine the overall defense process. The feedback and intense discussions during the initial panels led to the set of parameters that identifies an individual who has demonstrated a sufficient skill set for developing architectures.

The photograph in Figure 1.1 shows the first eight who worked on the development of the certification.

Figure 1.1   The first eight VCDX, shown at VMware Technical Summit 2008 (all VCDX Program Developers): John Arrasjid (#001), Mostafa Khalil (#002), Craig Risinger (#006), Enis Konuk, Melissa Tuite (Certification Program Manager), Andrew Hald (#004), Kamau Wanguhu (#003), Duncan Epping (#007), Richard Damoser (#008), and Mahesh Rajani (#005).

Photo credit: Thomas MacKay (Staff Systems Engineer)

Duncan Epping summarizes his experience:

> Back when VCDX was just released, Richard Damoser and I were the first to take the
> defense (after the original five developed and tested the concept). We did not know what to
> expect and were nervous for the unknown, but were also overly prepared. I took the exam in
> San Francisco during an internal training event and was still jet-lagged—having only slept
> for four hours in three days. That did not help. After every part of the defense, we were
> asked to leave the room; the panel members would decide if it even made sense to continue.
> If the panel felt there was no point in continuing, the defense would stop at that time. Even
> after the 15-minute presentation I prepared, I had to leave the room so that the panel could
> discuss my defense. Those ten minutes of waiting between the parts were difficult, and were
> taken out quickly as a result of the feedback of those defending that first week. I know my
> design was far from perfect, but that was no problem, as I had justification for it—some
> political, but most technical. That same week, during an award dinner, I had the honor to go
> up on stage and receive my certificate.

VMware Certification Program Framework

Although this book is geared toward individuals preparing for the final stages of VCDX
certification, it is important to understand that other certifications are prerequisites. Apologies in advance for the flood of acronyms in this chapter!

VMware certifications fall into separate solution tracks with multiple achievement levels:

- **Associate level:** VCA (VMware Certified Associate)
- **Professional level:** VCP (VMware Certified Professional)
- **Advanced Professional level:** VCAP (VMware Certified Advanced Professional)
- **Expert level:** VCDX (VMware Certified Design Expert)

Solution tracks include Datacenter Virtualization, End User Computing (desktop), Cloud,
and Cloud Application Platform. Newer certifications under development are role based,
with the content matched to job roles that include engineering, administration, architecture, development, and governance/operations. Note that the VMware VCA is not a
requirement in the VCDX program.

First, let's look at the original path that has developed into the VCDX-DCV, covering data center virtualization. This path involves validation of vSphere technology skills,
administration skills, and design skills through several stages of certification and a live
panel defense (see Figure 1.2).

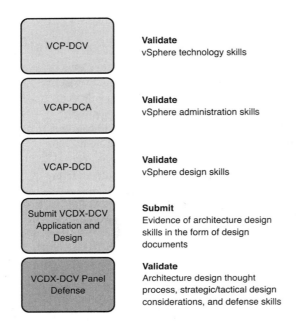

Figure 1.2   Example Datacenter Virtualization (VCDX-DCV) certification path.

VMware Certified Professional—Datacenter Virtualization (VCP-DCV) is the foundational VMware certification that focuses on technology, features, and operations of VMware vSphere.

VMware Certified Advanced Professional (VCAP) for vSphere offers certifications for various career tracks. The VCAP-DCA (Datacenter Administrator) leverages a remote lab to validate the hands-on skills administrators require. The VCAP-DCD (Datacenter Design) tests architecture skills and includes several design questions leveraging a custom modeling tool. Both VCAP-DCA and VCAP-DCD are required for the VCDX certification and can be completed in any order.

VMware Certified Design Expert (VCDX) is the highest level of VMware certification. This group comprises design architects highly skilled in architecture design who have demonstrated their expertise in designing VMware solutions.

Tips for the written exams:

- **Review the blueprint:** All content on the tests comes from the referenced materials in the test blueprint. Reading through the content might seem tedious, but you will be better prepared to take the exams. If you feel completely outmatched, consider taking a VMware education offering.

- **Set a date:** Imposing a date constraint provides motivation to work toward gaining the necessary experience to pass the exam. Fear of failure often contributes to procrastination and lack of progress.

- **Manage your time:** As with any standardized testing, allocate enough time to work through all the test questions. Do not fall into the trap of spending too much time on a single problem. The exception is the VCAP-DCD, where you should prioritize the design questions because of their higher weight.

- **Focus on feedback:** If you fail an exam, review the scoring to understand which areas require deliberate practice. Knowing what you don't know is the first step toward improvement.

Certification Tracks

Each solution track provides a progression from entry level, to the advanced professional level, and finally to the expert level.

Figure 1.3 illustrates the paths toward certification in the different solution tracks. The content is described broadly to provide guidance that applies to each track. Rules of inheritance enable a VCP in any track (Cloud, DCV, or DT) to sit for any DCD exam and achieve the underlying VCP certification for that track. For example, someone with VCP-Cloud could take the VCAP-DCD exam and achieve both results in VCP-DCV certification through inheritance.

Any VCP-level exam qualifies a candidate to sit any VCAP-level exams. Current VCDX holders in good standing may bridge to additional VCDX certifications by completing a two-step process. The first step is to complete both associated VCAP-level exams. The second step is to submit an application. When the application is accepted, the additional VCDX certification is awarded. All underlying certifications in the associated Solution Track are granted through the rules of inheritance.

The VCP-level certification has a prerequisite class, whereas the other certifications require VCP achievement. Check the VMware certification site for the full list of requirements. Each track has several related dependencies.

Pathways to VCDX Certification

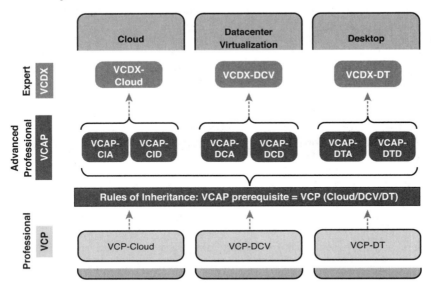

Figure 1.3   Certification Tracks.

Tips for VCAP-DCA test:

1. Review the blueprint—all possible test items are there (and more).

2. Get in the lab for hands-on experience, there is no substitution.

3. Complete the "creation" items first. These are fairly straightforward and simple. Make sure you do not skip any steps, because the test builds out sequentially. If dealing with long-running tasks (that is, maintenance mode or similar operations), work on other questions in parallel.

4. Focus on completing all tasks in which you have experience. If you have no clue about a particular item (that is, powerCLI scripting), go ahead and skip it. A perfect score is not required to pass.

5. Spend time on the troubleshooting items at the end. These require a bit more thought and tend to take up quite a bit of time.

VCDX for Datacenter Virtualization (VCDX-DCV)

VCDX for Datacenter Virtualization focuses on the core VMware virtualization technologies. VCP-DCV is the entry-level certification, with VCAP-DCA and VCAP-DCD at the advanced professional level. VCDX-DCV is the final certification representing the expert level.

Table 1.1 shows the level, the certification exam, the prerequisites, and the recommended classes for each level of the Datacenter Virtualization (DCV) track. The VCP-DCV level is the only one that requires a class before taking the exam.

Table 1.1 Datacenter Virtualization Track

Level	Exam	Prerequisites	Recommended Classes
Expert	VCDX-DCV	VCAP-DCA VCAP-DCD	VMware vSphere: Design Workshop
Advanced Professional (Design)	VCAP-DCD	VCP-DCV, DT, or Cloud	VMware vSphere: Design Workshop Business Continuity and Disaster Recovery Design
Advanced Professional (Administration)	VCAP-DCA	VCP-DCV, DT, or Cloud	VMware vSphere: Optimize and Scale
Professional	VCP-DCV	1. Attend a qualifying VMware authorized course. 2. Gain hands-on experience with VMware vSphere 5. 3. Pass the VCP5-DCV exam.	VMware vSphere: Install, Configure, Manage VMware vSphere: Fast Track VMware vSphere: Optimize and Scale VMware vSphere: What's New

VCDX for Desktop (VCDX-DT)

VCDX for Desktop focuses on the core technologies supporting desktop virtualization. A core component of this is the VMware View environment and the ThinApp technology. VCP-Desktop is the entry-level certification, with VCAP-DTA and VCAP-DTD at the advanced professional level. VCDX-DT is the final certification at the expert level.

Table 1.2 shows the level, the certification exam, the prerequisites, and the recommended classes for each level of the desktop (DT) track. The VCP-DT level is the only one that requires a class before taking the exam.

Table 1.2   Desktop Track

Level	Exam	Prerequisites	Recommended Classes
Expert	VCDX-DT	VCAP-DTD VCAP-DTA VCP-DT	
Advanced Professional (Design)	VCAP-DTD	VCP-DT, DCV, or Cloud	VMware View: Install, Configure, Manage Application Virtualization with VMware View VMware View: Design Best Practices
Advanced Professional (Administration)	VCAP-DTA	VCP-DT, DCV, or Cloud	
Professional	VCP-DT	1. Be a VCP-DCV. 2. Pass the VCP-DT exam.	VMware View: Install, Configure, Manage Application Virtualization with VMware View

Mock exams are essential in preparation and are recommend for evaluating your readiness before taking the real exam. Mock exams are available at http://www.vmware.com/certification.

VCDX for Cloud (VCDX-Cloud)

VCDX for Cloud focuses on the core technologies supporting cloud solutions. A core component of this is the VMware vCloud Suite. VCP-Cloud is the entry-level certification, with VCAP-CIA and VCAP-CID at the advanced professional level. VCDX-Cloud is the final certification at the expert level.

Table 1.3 shows the level, the certification exam, the prerequisites, and the recommended classes for each level of the cloud track. The VCP-Cloud level is the only one that requires a class before taking the exam.

Table 1.3 Cloud Track

Level	Exam	Prerequisites	Recommended Classes
Expert	VCDX-Cloud	VCAP-CID VCAP-CIA	
Advanced Professional (Design)	VCAP-CID	VCP-Cloud, DT, or DCV	VMware vCloud: Design Best Practices
Advanced Professional (Administration)	VCAP-CIA	VCP-Cloud, DT, or DCV	
Professional	VCP-Cloud	Path 1 1. Be a VCP-DCV. 2. Pass the IaaS exam. Path 2 1. Attend a qualifying course. 2. Pass the VCP-Cloud exam.	VMware vCloud: Deploy and Manage the VMware Cloud

The VCDX Process

After completing the prerequisite exams and gaining experience in creating designs for customers, you are ready to apply. The first step is to submit an application form for a scheduled panel defense. The flowchart in Figure 1.4 shows the sequence of events that can occur based on various outcomes.

When selecting a design, ensure that it is complex enough to support your depth and breadth of knowledge. A design for a small development environment with no SLAs might be technically sound, but it is less likely to reveal how a candidate can design for specific requirements and constraints. This is the reason the blueprint suggests a design that is suitable for business-critical applications in a production environment. No explicit sizing requirements exist, but consider that a 2-host cluster design does not allow for the same scoring opportunities as an 8- to 16-host cluster design with specific SLAs.

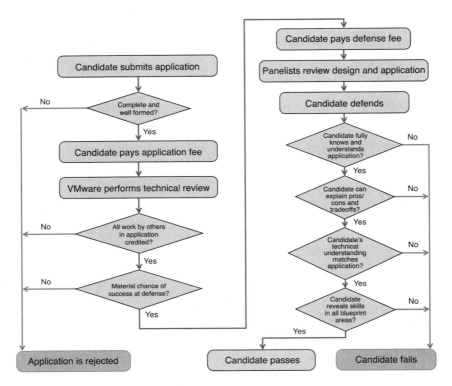

Figure 1.4 VCDX certification workflow.

Initial diagram by Brian Rice

When the design and supporting documents such as the test plan and operational procedures are finished, it is time to fill out the application. The VCDX Blueprint and the VCDX Handbook and application provide the requirements and full instructions for your submission. Additional details on how to complete the application are covered later in Chapter 2, "Preparation."

Application deadlines are set in advance of the actual defense dates. This provides enough time for both the initial application review and subsequent in-depth panelist reviews. Panelists review your materials and create a list of questions for use during the defense.

Value Proposition

Achieving VCDX certification has intrinsic and extrinsic benefits, depending on your motivation. Monetary or increased social media presence might be your main objective. Introspection of design skills could be another. Most commonly, you might be looking to challenge yourself. Whatever the case, most people who have gone through the process have found it to be a worthwhile learning experience.

Validating your capabilities to plan and design a VMware solution has tangible benefits to your career in terms of marketability, credibility, and compensation.

Benefits for VCDX holders include the following:

- VCDX certificate
- VCDX logo wear
- Use of the VMware Certified Design Expert logo on business cards and website
- Biography featured in the VCDX directory on VMware.com
- Discounted admission to VMware events
- Invitation to participate in beta classes and exams
- Invitation to participate in special events at VMworld-sponsored conferences
- Participation in VCDX communities
- Participation in the VCDX advisory board
- Additional benefits that may be one time or recurring, as defined by VMware

Wade Holmes (VCDX 15) talks about how achieving VCDX was just a starting point:

> Since joining VMware, my participation in the VCDX program has only helped to hone my skills as a virtualization and cloud architect. It has forced me to sharpen my understanding of enterprise architecture principles, principles that aid me greatly in my day-to-day role dealing with virtualization and cloud solutions. I will be forever grateful to the VCDX program in providing a vehicle that forced me to push myself and aiding me to take my career to another level.

Review

VMware's certification framework is structured along three solution tracks (Datacenter Virtualization, Desktop, and Cloud) and four levels: Associate, Professional, Advanced Professional, and Expert. Individuals who validate their skills by embarking on a certification path typically benefit from the recognition associated with achieving a particular level of certification. Certification requirements are subject to change. Visit http://www.vmware.com/certification for the latest information.

Chapter 2

Preparation

I fear not the man who has practiced 10,000 kicks once,
but I fear the man who has practiced one kick 10,000 times.

—Bruce Lee

The VMware Certified Design Expert (VCDX) is the highest level of VMware certification. It is a premier certification akin to the Cisco Certified Architect and other top-tier architecture certifications. The certification is geared towards veteran professionals who seek to demonstrate and validate their expertise as design architects developing virtualization, desktop, and cloud solutions. It measures a candidate's ability to design, implement, document, and validate a design using VMware technologies to meet customer objectives.

The VCDX Panel Defense is an oral interview consisting of three phases: a defense of the submitted design, a design scenario, and a troubleshooting scenario.

Candidates often approach us about the best way to prepare for the certification. This question has no catchall answer—it depends on the skills and experience of the candidate. What we *can* shed light on are the qualifications successful candidates demonstrate and, conversely, challenges that candidates who lack these qualifications face.

We assert that the majority of early certified individuals were intrinsically rather than extrinsically motivated. They chose to move forward with the certification process because of personal interests, not directives from management or the company.

Wade Holmes, VCDX-015, shares how he prepared:

> As an outsider looking in, the VCDX program was a goal that drove me to work on my craft and become a better architect. I had no idea what to expect when coming to defend and was extremely nervous. I spent countless hours preparing, reviewing my design, making sure I knew the ins and outs and could justify every granular detail I documented. Luckily, that was exactly the approach necessary for me to be successful. I can't describe how happy I was when I got a phone call that I passed and was a VCDX! (Yes, back then I was actually contacted by phone to be informed I had passed.)

Experience

One of the key differentiating factors that successful candidates possess is experience in designing a variety of complex architectures with enterprise customers. It is not enough to have experience; you need the right *type* of experience. Candidates typically have a background of several years in architecture design but are not limited to experience in the role of a datacenter architect. Individuals who have been certified include architects, consultants, technical support, sales systems engineers, and technical account managers. Job title doesn't matter—what counts is having spent time working on projects that developed the requisite skills.

Understanding enterprise architecture can be a valuable asset. Although knowledge of the frameworks and methodologies involved in a process is not required, it provides a broader perspective on architecture design. Throughout the process of design, design decisions must link back to the higher-level business goals that drive the overall solution capabilities. Tactical and strategic considerations are also important factors.

What Demonstrates Design Expertise?

Successful candidates invest significant time in aligning their design submission with the VCDX Blueprint and constantly reviewing the details of their design. Any aspect of the submitted material is fair game for questioning, so candidates spend a large amount of time preparing to defend all submitted material. For experienced consultants, this is no different from presenting a project summary to the customer at the end of an engagement. Being able to defend your design is an elemental skill of successful architects.

Consider spending time working with senior architects and reviewing designs from others to gain additional experience. Ask peers for constructive feedback to determine your strengths and weaknesses. Understanding deficiencies gives you the opportunity to seek appropriate training or experience, to improve your chances of succeeding.

Mastery of design considerations includes:

- Identifying and understanding business and technical requirements

- Identifying constraints and risks

- Understanding different enterprise architecture strategies

- Making and justifying design decisions

- Understanding the impact of design choices

- Knowing the implication of design choices, including the associated risks

During your design defense you should be able to:

- Provide a panelist with your solution, addressing requirements, constraints, and risks

- Answer all questions and defend your design choices

- Effectively manage your time, to demonstrate your ability to work effectively in design meetings with customers

We expect that candidates know their design but not necessarily know every component of the solution in excruciating detail. The following can put this in perspective:

> If you do not know the answer to a question, be honest about it. You can still try to explain how you think it works, but let them know that, in "real life," you would research this and come back to it as you would in a customer situation.
> —Duncan Epping, VCDX-007

What Demonstrates a Lack of Design Experience?

Most successful candidates have both deep architectural experience and strong technical skills. In most cases, when candidates do not successfully defend, it results from an inability to follow a common design approach, not from technical deficiencies. Designs that exhibit major technical flaws do not make it past the submission stage. We often hear the question, "How do I know when I'm ready to defend?" It sounds cliché, but if you are asking that question, you probably need more experience and confidence before you apply.

Insufficient mastery of design skills includes:

- A design that primarily focuses on delivery from templates, without addressing requirements

- Inability to articulate design decisions during the defense

    - Cannot understand or consider major aspects of a design

    - Cannot logically defend questions pertaining to a design decision

    - Does not demonstrate an understanding of the technologies included in the design

- Difficulty with starting a design process in front of a customer

- Inability to troubleshoot potential design or implementation issues

The Application

The VCDX Blueprint provides the areas covered during the review of submitted materials and the panel defense session. Carefully review the blueprint and ensure that your design is in alignment. In addition to the blueprint criteria, extensions can be included in the design, which might provide additional scoring opportunities, such as the following:

- Governance

- Multi-site considerations

- Risk analysis resolution

- Regulatory compliance

As an example, multi-site considerations are not mandatory but can provide additional opportunities for discussion that demonstrate a candidate's strengths. If the extensions are ultimately determined to be superfluous to the overall design goals and have incorrect components, this can have a negative impact. Extra content submitted should support the design and should reflect careful thought and review.

Carefully read the VCDX Blueprint and the VCDX Handbook and Application. Soliciting multiple reviews of your application package might be helpful, to ensure that you have included everything before you submit.

When planning for your prerequisite exams and budgeting time to work on your application, remember that applications should be ready approximately three months before the actual defense dates. This is due partly to deadlines, but also to the time and effort required to understand the application and complete the required material for submission.

Two registration fees are involved. One pays for the review of the application form and the technical review of the design by panelists. The second covers the actual defense session costs. Considering that three current VCDX-qualified architects painstakingly review your design, the cost is quite reasonable. As Michael Webster, VCDX-066, describes it, "This is the cheapest design review you'll ever get in your life!"

Application Submission Process

Complete the following steps for the actual panel defense.

1. Check the VCDX defense dates listed at http://www.vmware.com/go/vcdx. Use this to plan your timeline for preparation. Start early to ensure completeness and quality.

2. Download the latest versions of the VCDX Handbook, Application, and Blueprint.

3. Validate that your design matches the requirements in the VCDX Blueprint.

4. Request the defense date you prefer. If you have insufficient time, plan on a later date to complete your design, match the blueprints, and study all areas of the design.

5. Submit your completed application package to vcdx@vmware.com. This includes the completed application form, a signed attestation and statement of conduct, the documentation set, and the registration fee. This registration fee is for the initial review to determine whether the material demonstrates qualifications to sit for the VCDX defense.

6. The application is reviewed for completeness. Incomplete applications are returned to the applicant.

7. Accepted candidates receive confirmation of the complete application submission and an application fee payment link.

8. Upon receipt of payment, complete applications are advanced to the Technical Review phase.

9. Applications undergo a rigorous technical review by VCDX panelists.

   - Complete applications are reviewed for architecture design content (technical and operational).

   - Multiple individuals review and provide feedback on the content submitted. This takes up to four hours per design by up to three panelists.

10. The applicant receives the results of the Technical Review phase.

   ■ Accepted applicants receive an invitation to defend.

   ■ Rejected applicants receive a customized report of the top deficits in their design materials. This provides feedback on the topic area but does *not go* into detail on the deficits themselves.

11. Accepted applicants must confirm the date and time of their defense. The defense panel fee is due at this time.

VCDX Application

The VCDX Handbook provides instructions on the application and the process. The VCDX Blueprint provides the content areas that serve as the criteria for the design. Download the application and submit it with your design. The application is open to any individuals who meet the defined prerequisites.

Fictional Components

The submitted design can be fictitious, but you must be able to defend fictitious components. Designs that are entirely fictitious pose challenges to candidates, typically in the steps of conceptual and logical architecture design, and are *not* recommended. The panelists use the same standard for evaluation.

If content is missing for any VCDX Blueprint area, expand on your design to meet the missing areas or select another design for submission. This is an example of adding fictional components. Alignment of a design to the VCDX Blueprint provides a strong advantage because it demonstrates knowledge and skills required. The design must be consistent across both the documentation and the application. Missing blueprint items in your design minimize the scoring opportunities available and poses a risk to passing.

Designs that include fictitious components might be weak on listing requirements, constraints, assumptions, and risks. If fictional components are included, work on the details and have an architect review them. To be successful, understand all details of the design. Ensure that you provide these details in the design and are able to defend all of them.

Participation as an Architect

If the design is based on an actual project, you are required to have undertaken the architect role. While there may be multiple contributing architects, you are responsible for communicating areas beyond the part that you designed. In the application, document all contributors who worked on the design and their role.

Based on the experience of panelists, candidates who present a design that they had little involvement in tend to have major challenges in their panel defense session. Usually, these candidates cannot remember sufficient details, requirements, justification, impact, and risks.

Design for the VCDX Certification You Are Seeking

Each VCDX certification has a primary design component, as shown:

- VCDX-DCV primary component = VMware vSphere
- VCDX-DT primary components = VMware View
- VCDX-Cloud primary component = VMware vCloud Suite

Additional technologies may be included, such as VMware vCenter Site Recovery Manager, to cover the availability requirement in the blueprint. Remember that these additional areas open the door for more questioning by the panelists. This can lead to improved scoring opportunities, but it can also hurt scoring opportunities if a lack of understanding is exposed. Panels consist of individuals with a variety of different skill sets and specialties. As an example, you might submit a design with SRM included, and the panel might have extensive experience in SRM, mixed experience, or minimal experience. The experience level determines the level of questioning.

All design components included in the submission are subject to review and questioning under their relative scoring areas. When answering questions, focus on the requirements, constraints, assumptions, design considerations, and design patterns.

Be ready to answer any questions related to the submitted material. Failure to do so results in reduced scoring opportunities. This is an area where unprepared candidates typically face challenges. Know your design inside out!

Mandatory Documentation

A minimum set of documentation is required. The VCDX certification material includes the most current list. The Architecture Design, the Installation Guide, the Implementation Plan, the Testing Plan, and the Standard Operating Procedures are covered here. All documentation must align with the submitted design. Some candidates lose scoring opportunities by using generic test plans that do not support the details of the design or are not specific to the customer.

- The *Architecture Design* includes the following as a minimum: logical design, physical design, diagrams, requirements, constraints, assumptions, and risks. As part of this, justifications and implications of design considerations included in the documentation typically provide an advantage to the candidate.

- The *Installation Guide* should include instructions on installation steps specific to the overall design. This includes items beyond the core components.

- The *Implementation Plan* should include roles, responsibilities, timelines, and deployment guidance specific to the overall design.

- The *Testing (or Validation) Plan* considers the overall design. Perform both unit-level testing (ULT) and system-level testing (SLT) to validate individual components and integration points between these components. References to vendor integration guidelines and validation should be included where appropriate. This can include compatibility guides and integration-level testing (ILT).

- The *Standard Operating Procedures* provide the recurring operating procedures for the design submitted.

VCDX panelists review your application and the documentation submitted. Qualified design experts prevalidate a candidate during this review. They create questions for the defense and identify both strengths and weaknesses. These questions guide the defense session and validate the candidate's skills. If details are missing, the reviewers cannot guess what they are.

Use of best practices may apply for a majority of implementations, but these are not customer specific or applicable in all situations. A qualified design expert knows when to deviate from a best practice while providing a justifiable and supportable solution. Michael Webster, VCDX-066, elaborates on this point:

> Best practices are a baseline from which we work in the absence of specific requirements that would justify deviation. Knowing why it is a best practice is important so that you know where to create a new best practice specific to your design and customer.

Consider that best practices provide the best approach to implementing a specific feature or function for a given, or predetermined, scenario. If your customer requires modification to the best practice, provide the customer-specific best practice, with supporting details.

Strict confidentiality of candidate materials is enforced. Access to their materials is restricted to those involved in prereview and in the panel defense. This material is used to generate questions for use in the defense. All submitted material is removed within a specific internal, legally required window of time.

Creating a VCDX Study Group

A study session benefits from different perspectives and points of view. When setting up a study session, identify other candidates at or above your current progress. We recommend that the study group you select includes individuals who have completed the VCAP design-level certification for the VCDX defense you are attempting. As a group, help each other work through challenges and provide feedback to improve designs and develop your scenario skills.

Practice and Supporting Materials

Focus study sessions on design content, design defense, and scenarios. Several scenarios are included as examples to use during your study session, to practice your skills.

- Review designs for alignment with VCDX Blueprints.

- Have each candidate delivers his or her presentation.

- Have other group members ask questions on the design areas chosen by a candidate.

- Use the scenarios provided in this book to simulate the design and troubleshooting scenario sections.

- Have the panelists review a candidate's design and generate a list of questions.

- Have the panelists review scenarios used to determine solution areas that will validate the skills of the VCDX candidate.

- Review Chapter 4, "Defense Overview," and the section on the VCDX Panel Defense participants, to understand the roles of everyone who participates in a defense session. The next section outlines specific guidelines for soliciting VCDX panelists to run or participate in a VCDX Boot Camp or Study Session.

VCDX Panelist Restrictions

VCDX panelists are not permitted to review or comment on a design outside their assigned VCDX defense reviews or as part of their work assignments. The best way to leverage active panelists is to have them conduct a VCDX panel defense boot camp that does not go into specifics about a candidate's design.

Panelists cannot mentor candidates. This includes providing feedback on a candidate application form or submitted materials. A panelist can participate in VCDX panel defense boot camps that focus on providing guidelines for success, but they must not go into details that would provide an unfair advantage to a candidate. Preparation workshops run by VCDX panelists can cover only the information in the official VCDX preparation workshop material available on VMware.com.

Running a VCDX Panel Defense Boot Camp

A defense boot camp covers material from this book and uses a variation of the boot camp slide deck available at http://www.vmware.com/go/vcdx.

Panelists can run a boot camp without going into specific design feedback. They can provide high-level feedback during the design and troubleshooting scenarios.

Practice

A mock defense is similar to a real defense.

- A similar environment is created with a white board, a projector, a timing device, and participants.

- One person is designated the moderator, to manage the clock.

- Three people (if possible) act as panelists. They review the candidate's design and create questions for the candidate. More than three people can participate as panelists during this mock defense.

- Stick to the time constraints, and do not provide a time extension.

- Focus on asking questions tied to the VCDX Design Blueprint and relevant areas in the design.

Room Layout

The room layout should look similar to Figure 2.1.

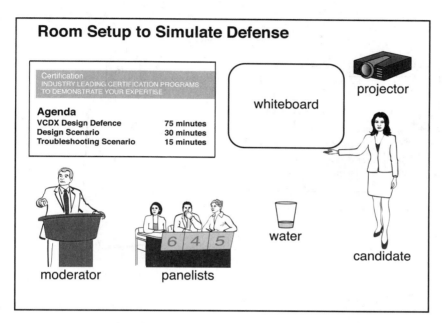

Figure 2.1   Mock defense room setup.

Take advantage of all available instruments: the whiteboard, the projector with presentations and scenarios, and the panelists, as illustrated in Figure 2.2. If possible, use two projectors to ease the process of working through the design and troubleshooting scenarios.

Voicing your thought process is critical for displaying your design methodology to the panelists. Doing so may also preemptively answer questions that the panelists have formulated, saving time for other scoring opportunities.

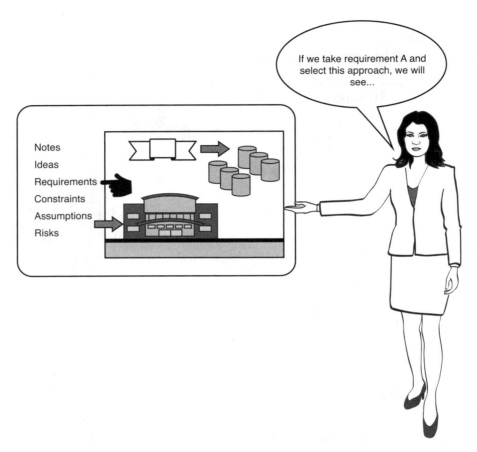

Figure 2.2 Thinking aloud and using the whiteboard.

Running the Defense Within a Set Timeline

The moderator sets up a timer. This can be as simple as a watch or stopwatch, or a custom-designed timer similar to that used in the actual defense.

Here is a recommended timeline:

- Set up the room = 20 to 30 minutes
- Conduct Design Defense = 75 minutes
- Break = 15 minutes

- Conduct Design Scenario = 30 minutes for VCDX-DCV, 45 minutes for VCDX-Cloud and VCDX-DT

- Conduct Troubleshooting Scenario = 15 minutes for VCDX-DCV, 30 minutes for VCDX-Cloud and VCDX-DT

- Discuss feedback with the candidate = 30 to 45 minutes

Mock Defense Checklist

☐ Identify participants.

    ☐ Recommended: 1 candidate, 3 mock panelists, 1 moderator

    ☐ Minimal: 1 candidate, 1 mock panelist/moderator

☐ Provide a timer.

☐ Have mock panelists review the candidate's design and create questions (completed before the mock defense).

☐ Select a design scenario to use (matched to the chosen VCDX certification).

☐ Select a troubleshooting scenario to use (matched to the chosen VCDX certification).

☐ Run the defense following the rules and timelines defined.

☐ Ensure that the timer used is visible to both the panelists and the candidate.

☐ Provide water or other refreshments.

Review

Use the following checklist to determine your readiness:

☐ Can you identify and understand all business requirements and demonstrate how they are addressed in the design?

☐ Can you explain each decision and defend the choice?

☐ Can you discuss other possible options and justify why you made the choice that you did?

- ☐ Do you have experience in all areas and technologies that the design covers?
- ☐ Have you selected a design that matches the requirements of the blueprint and the application?
- ☐ Did you use best practices and understand why they are best practices for the project at hand?
- ☐ Can you identify areas where you deviated from best practices? Can you defend why you did so?
- ☐ Did you provide a complete solution to meet the business requirements?
- ☐ Can you identify the constraints imposed?
- ☐ Can you identify the risks inherent in the design, the likelihood of the risk occurring, and the mitigation steps?
- ☐ Do you have a concept of enterprise architecture strategies?
- ☐ Have you validated that all decisions are sound and that you understand their impact on other areas of the design or the project, such as budget, required skills, timelines, and technologies?
- ☐ Can you answer all questions panelists raise?
- ☐ Have you run your own study session, boot camp, or mock defense with others?
- ☐ Can you effectively manage your time in a high-pressure, time-sensitive defense session?
- ☐ Can you whiteboard your design with all relevant components?

Chapter 3

The Design

Good design is good business.

—Thomas Watson, Jr.

The proficiency displayed in the application package determines whether a candidate is offered the opportunity to defend. Words and diagrams poured into the design are the first impression made to prospective panelists and the element that you have the most control over. Most critical is the architecture design document, the keystone piece that drives the other components. Invest the time to ensure completeness and accuracy of the submitted design, as this translates into time saved in the design defense. Strive for maximum readability and flow through the submitted material.

Prospective candidates often ask about the required complexity of the submitted design. There is no stated requirement on the number of pages in the design document or the approximate size of the solution. However, common sense dictates that a smaller scale design makes it difficult to demonstrate architectural skills. Enterprise scale is an ideal, a solution that necessitates the participation of numerous stakeholders and architects. Select a design with sufficient complexity that demonstrates the depth and breadth of knowledge and skills relevant to designing a solution.

Assembling Your Design

When starting a design, review the appropriate blueprint areas. Ensure that your design decisions are aligned with the requirements and constraints. A printout and a red pen come in handy here. Multiple reviews help identify areas of accomplishment and areas of deficiencies. If you do not find any weak points, solicit a trusted peer to review your work. Afterward, adjust your design to improve the weak areas. Rinse, repeat.

> **TIP**
>
> If your design violates best practices or seems dubious in some way, explain your rationale to avoid point deductions.

VCDX Design Defense Blueprint

The Design Defense Blueprint is your guide to the process and requirements to achieve certification. The VMware certification website has a unique blueprint for each VCDX variant.

Blueprint Outline

Here is a summary of the major sections of the blueprint[1]. Refer to the blueprint for your defense version for details.

- Purpose and structure of the VCDX certification
- Intended audience
- The application and defense
  - Format and structure of the defense
  - Procedures and policies
- Objectives covered in the design defense
- VCDX paths and supporting courses
- Path from customer requirements, to solution architecture, to engineering specifications (see Figure 3.1)

---

[1]Subject to change and update. See http://vmware.com/certification for the most current information and requirements.

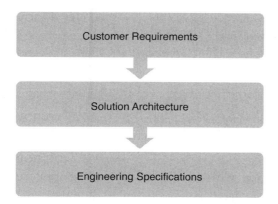

Figure 3.1   Customer requirements → solution architecture → engineering specifications.

- Customer requirements (supports the conceptual model)
- Solution architecture (logical architecture)
- Engineering specifications (physical architecture)
- Implementation guidance—includes the following:
  - Deployment plan
  - Installation guide
  - Standard operating procedures
  - Validation and test plan

This blueprint is a starting point that outlines the requirements and provides foundational guidance for maximum scoring potential.

Core components of a submitted design include a design document that presents requirements and an architectural solution. Supporting material includes an installation guide to match the design along with a validation plan. Provide more than just basic items. A simple test plan may miss important validation steps that could result in failure of the implementation.

Those with access to design templates should remember that these are a starting point and do not include a full set of requirements and constraints that determine the final architecture. Use of service delivery templates[2] does not guarantee success. Providing a complete design that meets the blueprint areas is what determines your results.

---

[2]Teams use service delivery templates as a starting point for designs.

Panelists spend approximately four hours reviewing each application and submitted documents. That potentially adds up to twelve hours of review time per candidate! They inspect all documentation and develop clarifying questions for use during the design defense.

What Panelists Look For

> Know why you chose to use a specific option; understand why you did not choose the other available options.
> —Frank Denneman, VCDX-029

First, panelists look at design requirements, constraints, assumptions, and risks. Subsequently, they review the design, looking for design decisions and patterns that support the requirements and constraints. Aspects such as consistency, accuracy, and supportability of the design are considered.

Include requirements, constraints, assumptions, and risks in a dedicated document or within the architecture design document. One approach is to create an indexed table for each of these categories to simplify referencing.

The submitted design and related documents should include:

- Compute
- Networking
- Storage
- vCenter Server
- ESXi server
- Virtual machines
- Security
- Business continuity and disaster recovery
- Monitoring
- Upgrades
- Capacity planning
- Standard operating procedures
- Additional management components

Submit a sufficiently complex design that demonstrates architectural skill. Doing so often leads to interesting conversations that can lead to higher levels of success.

> The more you can include in your design, the better conversations can be had with the panelists. Your goal isn't necessarily to wow the panel with your documented solution as much as demonstrate your ability to take requirements and generate a solution.
> —Doug Baer, VCDX-019

Using "best practices" requires you to know the background behind the best practice and how it applies to this situation. This is not a knock on best practices since they are a useful pattern in designing large infrastructures. As designs evolve, best practices may follow. If you have a customized design best practice, provide the support (that is, examples from past work experience).

> The answer to a question can never be 'because it is a best practice'—know why this is a best practice, and know why it met the requirements of your customer!
> —Duncan Epping (VCDX-007)

Validation and test plans justify the implementation, ensuring it functions as expected. These typically include testing of the virtualization platform, management tools, infrastructure components, and advanced features used. If you add design-related material for other VMware technology areas, include installation and validation plans for them. Validation plans can include functional, performance, and utilization considerations.

NOTE

Ask yourself, "Can I give this documentation to my customer and have them perform the deployment themselves?" If not, the documentation is not comprehensive enough. Align the implementation guide and standard operational procedures with the overall design.

If using unique design patterns and best practices, provide the justification and impact. Call out the creative approach during the defense overview presentation. Top performers consider extensions to the design to meet additional blueprint requirements. This can be a slippery slope, as you are responsible for justifying all content in the application.

Method

Today, there is no published standard architectural method when it comes to virtualization and VMware technologies. Internally, there are several frameworks under continuous development. Gradually these frameworks have de-emphasized technological aspects while adopting elements of software design and enterprise architecture. The method in Figure 3.2 describes a framework that has proven helpful in developing an architecture specific to a customer's needs.

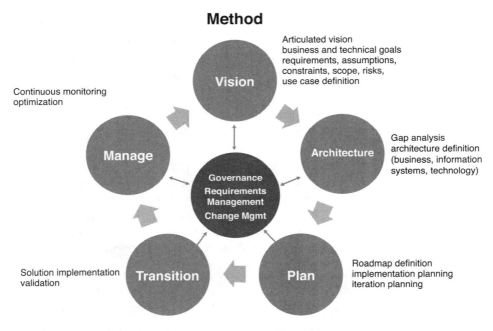

Figure 3.2   Phases for developing customer-specific architecture.

At the outset, the *Vision* phase outlines the overall business goals, architecture scope, and key stakeholders. The baseline and target states for the architecture may be described here.

In the *Architecture* phase, the logical design is constructed through analysis of requirements and constraints collected from various stakeholders.

The *Plan* phase covers the physical implementation details for deploying the architecture. Depending on the scope of the project, the architecture is built and validated in one or more *Transition* phases.

Finally, the *Manage* phase covers proactive monitoring and management of the deployed architecture.

In all phases, there is periodic validation of project outputs to requirements. New requirements or technology might necessitate a design change. Architecture design is an iterative process, over the entire method in one or more transition phases.

Traceability

A signature of good designs is the linkage of design choices back to high-level goals. The first step is categorizing and prioritizing various customer inputs. After capturing the inputs, map design decisions to business requirements, technical requirements, or constraints. Document assumptions and risks, especially if they will have a significant impact on a design. Good organization is essential when developing a complex and thorough design. Tables 3.1 and 3.2 provide examples of categorizing requirements and constraints.

Table 3.1 Categorizing Requirements

#	Title	Description
R101	Portal	The consumer has the ability to deploy services from a catalog.
R102	Portal	Expose an API for end users.
R103	Service Tiers	The system provides two tiers of service: tier 1 for production workloads and tier 2 for development/test.
R104	Networking	Provide each tenant with a direct network connection and the capability to provision multiple isolated networks.
R105	Catalog	Provide a global catalog of templates and ISO media.

Table 3.2 Categorizing Constraints

#	Title	Description
C101	Server	The target host is a blade server (16 cores, 64 GB memory, 2 CNAs[1]).
C102	Cluster	The total number of hosts is 16 (4 per chassis).
C103	Storage	The target storage array is FC (gold) and iSCSI (silver) storage.
C104	Network	Available network bandwidth is 10 Gbps.
C105	Billing	An existing internal billing system is used.

[1] A converged network adapter (CNA) is a computer I/O device that has both host bus adapter (HBA) and network interface controller (NIC) functionality. In most cases, this is a convergence of a computer network with a storage-area network.

Resolving Conflicts

At some point, conflicts in the pool of requirements, constraints, assumptions, and risks may exist. Let's look at how these relate to each other and consider how to resolve conflict.

Some candidates create a table of all major design decisions that reference the section and page in the submitted material that contains further details. This approach offers multiple benefits. It is easier for a customer, a reviewer, and the panelists to identify the decisions made and locate the supporting material. Remember, a table does not replace documentation. Other reference information can include tables of figures, diagrams, and data tables.

Requirements

Requirements describe, in business or technical terms, the necessary properties, qualities, and characteristics of a solution. Customers provide requirements that form the basis for the design. If particular requirements cannot be met, they are marked accordingly in the appropriate section of the following table and further in the documentation. Use a consistent approach for documenting requirements. This simplifies identification and cross referencing.

Sometimes requirements conflict. For example, a customer requirement may state that the disaster recovery site support the same Service Level Agreements (SLAs) as the primary site. Another requirement stipulates an RPO of five minutes and an RTO of one hour. Address and resolve design conflicts. Requirements can evolve through discussion and negotiation. Documentation on these changes supports traceability and accountability. Include the justification and impact of the changes.

Constraints

Constraints can limit the design features and the implementation of the design. The most common example is a customer sticking with a preferred vendor or preexisting technology. Constraints influence requirements for the project, requiring compromise.

> Think about the constraints in your current design and which changes you would have made if these constraints were lifted.
> —Frank Denneman, VCDX-029

Without constraints, design would be easier but also much less interesting. Think of constraints as challenges, rather than barriers. How distinctive would Twitter be without the 140 character limit?

Assumptions

> Erroneous assumptions can be disastrous.
> —Peter Drucker

Assumptions are expectations made during the design phase about the implementation and use of a system. Since assumptions cannot be confirmed initially, they pose risks to the design if left unaddressed. They are implied by the requirements, constraints, standards, experience, and best practices used. Examples include hardware/software compatibility requirements or sufficient network bandwidth needed to support an expected performance level.

> In the absence of factual information, you may need to make an assumption. This should be an educated guess and preferably based upon other available factual information or evidence. For example, if you are building a new vCloud Datacenter offering, how do you know how many concurrent users might connect to each vCloud Director cell? You don't! So you have to make an educated guess (assumption) based on experience, add it to a risk register, and have a mitigation plan in place for if your guess proves incorrect. In this case, the mitigating action(s) could be that you over deploy the number of vCloud Director cells or that you simply monitor the concurrent users and deploy when load exceeds the desired threshold. It then falls into the operational/capacity planning activities to manage this moving forward. Not all assumptions need to be validated in order to complete a design, but they do need to be managed.
> —Aidan Dalgleish, VCDX-010

Risks

Risks may negatively impact the reliability of the design. This can include people, process, or technology risk. For instance, lack of training may hinder day-to-day operations, whereas a single point of failure in the solution stack impacts SLAs. Document risks to the project along with the appropriate mitigations.

Sizes Matters Not

Some submitted designs have exceeded 500 pages; others consist of less than 200 pages. Again, there is no minimum or maximum page requirement. Reflect on your experience and surmise what an enterprise customer expects from a fully fledged plan and design service engagement.

If using pre-existing design templates, we expect customization of templates to meet the blueprint requirements and ensure that all design decisions, patterns, and impacts are captured. Adding superfluous content to pad a design document is not always a wise strategy. The design should provide a solution architecture that meets the customer's requirements and constraints.

Design Artifacts

The text and diagrams that accompany your design serve to elaborate on core design principles and decisions. Simplicity and purity are favored over glitz. What matters is being able to convey the rationale behind a decision, not a fancy diagram that detracts from readability. Useful diagrams are unobtrusive, self-explanatory ways to clarify structure.

What Makes for a Good Design?

A good design meets requirements with the appropriate technology and operational guidance to match a schedule, staffing requirements, and budget. Understanding and documenting the reasons for each decision must factor in the requirements, the constraints, and the technology influencing the solution.

When developing design decisions and design patterns, consider those that go beyond simplistic and standard choices. One example is to extend basic NIC redundancy by providing details on the use of load-based teaming, network I/O control, or Link Aggregation (LACP) on a distributed switch.

Include the conceptual model, logical design, and physical design. Successful candidates include all three in their design. The conceptual model maps the requirements and constraints used to influence the logical design. The logical design provides the platform to make technology choices. The physical design provides the details and configurations of the technologies used.

Although candidates have passed without demonstrating a formal progression from conceptual models to logical and physical designs, we recommend that you include all three to provide better insight into your design strategy and progression in developing the solution.

Conceptual Model

The conceptual model of the design includes customer requirements and constraints. It also includes assumptions that are implied and relevant to the design.

When creating the design, map requirements, constraints, and assumptions into one or more of the following design qualities.

1. **Availability**

   Requirement: Deliver highly available operation, as measured by percent uptime of relevant components.

2. **Manageability**

   Requirement: Provide ease of managing the environment and maintaining normal operations. Subqualities may include scalability and flexibility.

3. **Performance**

   Requirement: Deliver the standards of responsiveness of components of the desired environment to meet the application workloads deployed and SLAs specified.

4. **Recoverability**

   Requirement: Provide the capability to recover from an unexpected incident that affects the availability of an environment.

5. **Security**

   Requirement: Provide overall data control, confidentiality, integrity, accessibility, governance, and risk management, often including the capability to demonstrate or achieve compliance with regulation.

These five design qualities apply to each VCDX track, as illustrated in Figure 3.3.

The panel looks for your ability to build relationship models among the design components to create solutions based on these mappings. The models include, but are not limited to, components involving the following:

- Cloud, desktop, and/or virtual datacenter management technologies based on the intended VCDX track
- Computing resources
- Storage resources
- Networking resources
- Virtual machines and vApps

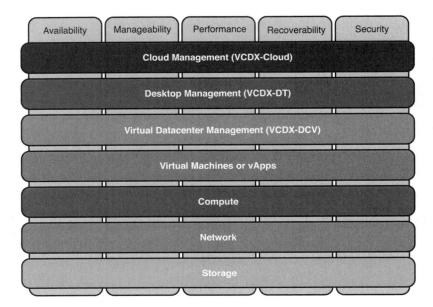

Figure 3.3   Relationship models.

Logical Design

Recognize that "logical" does not mean "physical" where the physical implementation details are included. For VCDX, we have acknowledged a hybrid approach with known constraints, including the use of VMware vSphere as an underlying component. This is acceptable. If you specify versioning information (that is, VMware vSphere 5.1), you are now providing configuration and versioning details that constitute a physical design. Understand that the progression from conceptual, to logical, to physical demonstrates the journey you take from the abstract vision to the specific details. Focus on the conceptual and logical levels first to ensure that the final physical design meets the requirements for expected functional results. A hybrid approach will not result in deductions as long as the candidate understands that this is a mixture of logical with some physical design elements.

Most successful candidates include both the logical and the physical design components.

- They provide guidance on how the logical design relates to the requirements.

- They address the selection of the physical components to meet the logical design.

- They provide a physical design that guides the implementation process.

Physical Design

The physical design includes the implementation details, including choice of vendors and technologies. This is where the logical design turns into a design specification for implementation. We recommend including a "Bill of Material" that lists the software and hardware components along with any necessary training necessary.

Justification

What compelling requirement, constraint, assumption, or risk mitigation drove your decisions?

"Just because" or "it is a best practice" opens the door to questioning your abilities as an architect. Best practices are not set in stone—nor are they the only option. Best practices evolve over time to meet specific use cases but may not be the best practice for all.

Panelists can ask for clarification on the best practice and details on why it is a best practice for the specific project. Validate the modified best practice, and show the impact of the change. Your justifications demonstrate support of the requirement and value of the solution.

Ensure that the decisions made concerning conflicts include justification, approval, and impact to other areas of the design. Incorrect design decisions influenced by weak requirements can lead to lower scoring. To score higher, provide details on conflicting requirements. Call out the choices made for each requirement. Provide details and merits of an alternative set of requirements that resolve the conflict.

Impact

How did the decision affect other areas of the design with respect to technology, risk, schedule, skills, budget, or other critical areas?

Justification does not equal impact. Impact can be both positive and negative. A higher cost might provide a more resilient solution and reduce risk. The return on investment (ROI) demonstrates the positive versus the negative. It includes financial, technical, and other components that could be affected by the decision.

Localization

Currently, application documents must be submitted in English. If you translate from another language to English, consider adding English reviewers to ensure correct translation of concepts. Translators and translation programs could differ in their final wording.

Perform design validation before submitting. This could include peer review, running a mock panel defense, or practicing with others by defending your design in English.

Checklist: Design Selection and Content

☐ Aligned with VCDX Blueprint

☐ Includes design considerations

☐ Includes design patterns

☐ Includes justifications

☐ Includes impact of design choices on other areas

☐ Includes risk analysis and mitigations

☐ Includes content beyond a basic template

☐ Reviewed by others to identify strengths and weaknesses

Summary

The completeness and accuracy of the application package is the best way to improve your chances at a successful defense. While the actual defense flies by in roughly two hours, candidates have worked on their designs for weeks and months. As panelists, it is easy to predict which candidates will be successful based on the strength of your documentation alone. Focus your time wisely, draw on your experience, seek guidance from advisors, and submit an application that displays your proficiency as an architect.

There are three phases covered in the development of a design. The first phase is the development of a conceptual model that maps the requirements and constraints used to influence the logical design. The logical design provides the platform to make technology choices. The physical design includes the implementation details with specific vendor, product, and configuration information.

Within a design, consider the justification and impact of a design choice. Justification supports a decision. Impact is the result of a decision. Justification can result in either a positive or a negative impact. Impact of a design choice occurs in other areas than the decision point. Impact can affect budget, technology, training, and other decisions. Consider each of the items above when developing your design for submission. The panel looks at how you address these phases in your design and how each design choice is justified.

In this section, we illustrated the steps to developing a design submission. The following is a checklist to help prepare for your defense. Several of these are detailed in their relevant chapters.

- ☐ Understand the timing and flow of the panel defense.
- ☐ Understand the requirements for the design defense (Chapter 5).
- ☐ Understand the requirements for the design scenario (Chapter 6).
- ☐ Understand the requirements for the troubleshooting scenario (Chapter 7).
- ☐ Know all aspects of your design.

Chapter 4

Defense Overview

Before anything else, preparation is the key to success.

—Alexander Graham Bell

The VCDX defense evaluates the capabilities of the candidate through the following:

- Demonstrating architecture skills through defense of the submitted design
- Designing from scratch through a design scenario
- Troubleshooting issues resulting from a design or implementation flaw

This chapter is an overview of the defense process. Subsequent chapters cover three major acts in more detail. Chapter 5 covers the design defense, Chapter 6 covers the design scenario, and Chapter 7 covers the troubleshooting scenario.

The Interview Process

The interview consists of your design defense (75 minutes) and two role-play scenarios: the design scenario (30 or 45 minutes) and the troubleshooting scenario (15 or 30 minutes). The VCDX-DCV allocates 30 minutes to the design scenario and 15 minutes to the troubleshooting scenario. The VCDX-Cloud and VCDX-DT allocate 45 minutes to the design scenario and 30 minutes to the troubleshooting scenario. There is a short break between the design defense and the scenarios.

Maintain a good mental state when working through your defense. Clear thinking is required. Although you might be under stress during the defense, remember that the panelists were in your position previously. They are individuals like you and are there to evaluate your skills, just as you might evaluate the skills of others in your field.

Before the Defense

Get plenty of rest before you show up, especially if you have a morning defense. Most candidates arrive early—some too early. Plan to arrive 10 to 20 minutes before the start time. Arrive any earlier, and you might psych yourself out. Do not show up in a sleep-deprived state. At this point, you should have spent a good amount of time studying your design carefully. Give your body the needed rest to conduct your defense with confidence.

Nerves are always a factor, even for the most experienced architects. Although the panelists look as if they are positioned strategically to induce the maximum amount of stress (opposite yourself), this is merely to protect the contents of their laptops. We have seen a few candidates become visibly flustered from the sheer stress of the situation.

Holding a mock defense is a simple way to address this stress. It allows you to acclimate to the pressure of defending your design, boosting your confidence. Finding a panel of peers is ideal, even if it is easier to schedule members of your household (although the latter might be a tougher crowd). Refer to Chapter 2, "Preparation," for more details.

Practicing your design defense in front of an audience is important. Plan for this well in advance of your panel defense. Select individuals who will throw rocks at your design choices and the documents you submit. The mock defense panel does not have to be the most technical audience, but they should be able to ask critical questions and act like a customer.

Time Management

Once in the flow of the defense, time seems to elapse faster than usual. This is normal. The rapid-fire questioning enables the panelists to assess your strength in specific areas outlined in the blueprint.

The panelists expect consistency in your approach during each phase of the defense. Do not waste time on things that are irrelevant; you have only a short amount of time, and it is paramount that you use it wisely. If you do not know something, simply say that you don't know and move on so you can have the best chance of scoring more points in the time allocated. Feel free to take a best guess (making clear it is only a guess), to demonstrate what knowledge you do have and how you can think logically. This is important—if you just say "I don't know," you do not gain any points, whereas you might get considerable credit for demonstrating what you do know and how well you reason. When the clock runs out, your time is up.

Panel Defense Participants

The Panel Defense is an interview between the candidate and a panel of VCDX-certified architects. The participants for each defense include panelists, observers, and moderators. They are responsible for the following:

Panelists:

- Assess the candidate's skills

- Cannot discuss the candidate's performance or results with others

- Interact with the candidate

- Record scores based on the scoring rubric

Depending on the phase of the defense, panelists act as either your peers or a customer. When they are acting as a customer, they might act as if they do not have certain information or do not know certain things, just like a real customer.

Observers:

- Sometimes are called "panelists in training" and do not actively participate in the defense

- Cannot discuss the candidate's performance or results with others

- Participate to learn how to conduct the defense

- Do not interact with the candidate

- Do not affect a candidate's score

Moderators:

- Act as a timekeeper

- Ensure that the session is conducted in a professional and objective manner following the defined rules for a panel defense

Environment

The moderator maintains a timer made visible to both you and the panelists. The timer pauses between sections of the defense. Initially a free online timer was used before Andrew Mitchell, VCDX-030, took it upon himself to develop a more professional looking tool.

The room contains a whiteboard or drawing apparatus, one to two projectors, and a laptop for showing your presentation.

Backpacks, cell phones, laptops, and other nonessential material are not permitted in the room. They are stored in a designated secure area until the completion of the defense.

During your defense, do not interpret facial expressions or body gestures of the panelists. If a panelist is nodding, frowning, or yawning, this is not a reflection on your defense. It does not reflect positively or negatively on a given answer or your performance in general.

The panelists might ask follow-up questions. These are intended to probe your skills for further scoring opportunities, not to try to find your weaknesses.

Make sure you are comfortable in your surroundings, including elements such as room temperature and space. If you need adjustments or have other requests, ask the moderator.

The moderator will provide beverages. Talking for three hours is thirsty work!

Panelists' Perspective

This section covers the panelists' roles, qualifications, preparation, and expectations.

Sitting in the Panelist Seat

> Remember, the panelists are pretending to be uneducated customers for the scenarios. You need to forget what they know and justify your recommendations.
> —Chris Colotti, VCDX-037

Understanding the perspective of the panelists is important. You might think there is magic behind the scenes, but in reality, panelists use precise validated tools to determine a candidate's overall performance.

The goal of panelists is to expand the community of VCDX-certified individuals. We believe that the certification is *not* limited to architects. We believe, and have proven, that individuals with other backgrounds can learn the skills and achieve the certification.

Remember that panelists are the only scoring individuals in the room. Direct your points to these three individuals during the defense. The observers do not talk: They participate to learn the process and validate their understanding of the training. The moderator focuses on ensuring that everyone keeps to the schedule and follows the rules.

Panelist Qualifications

> Panelists are experts in various virtualization areas. Don't make technology claims that are incorrect and expect to talk yourself out of it.
> —Duncan Epping, VCDX-007

Panelists must hold a current VCDX certification and complete the requisite number of hours training as a Panel Defense observer. Observers go through the same scoring process to validate alignment with the seasoned panelists.

Panelists must focus on the minimally qualified candidate as defined by the program materials and the panelist guidelines. Panelists are current in their VMware knowledge and skills.

Panelist Preparation

The panelists for a particular defense session prepare by reviewing the materials each candidate submits. As part of this review, the panelists formulate questions and areas for deeper exploration in the defense.

The panelists discuss areas to cover during the defense. They might discuss questions they plan to ask.

Panelist Expectations

Panelists expect you to show the path you took from start to finish for the scenarios. They do not expect you to design a complete solution or determine the root cause during the scenarios phase of the defense. Demonstrate your architecture design approach and how to resolve the conflict or problems.

Notification of Results

After the panel defense is complete, the certification team works to provide results as soon as possible. When scoring is finalized and entered into the certification system, you will receive the results via e-mail in approximately ten business days.

A report of failure includes high-level feedback on the most significant areas affecting the outcome. Notification of passing includes the assignment of a unique VCDX number, a certificate, and the option to add your biography to the online VCDX Directory.

Chapter 5

Design Defense

*If you can't explain it to a six-year-old,
you don't understand it yourself.*

—Albert Einstein

The Design Defense is 75 minutes long and provides an opportunity to present and defend your submitted design to a panel of architects.

Prior to the defense, prepare the following.

- A presentation for the panel that outlines key aspects of your design.

- USB key or other media containing your presentation in Microsoft PowerPoint or SlideRocket format.

Do not bring additional items or props for the defense. When arriving at the session, personal items such as laptops, cell phones, and other items will be stored in a secured location.

Bringing printed copies of the design into the room is not permitted. Include design references as part of the presentation slide deck. Note that panelists, observers, and the moderator cannot accept gifts or promises of alcohol from the candidate. You wouldn't bribe your test proctor, would you? We do appreciate the gesture though!

When the presentation is loaded and ready, the moderator reads several prepared remarks covering the guidelines of the defense. After the moderator activates the timer, the floor is yours. Do not be overwhelmed by the situation. Do not over think it. Organize your thoughts and focus intently.

The time requirements are adhered to using a web-based timer. Figure 5.1 shows an example of this timer.

Design Defense

75:00

Figure 5.1   The rather expensive VCDX timer.

Design Overview Presentation

The defense phase begins with a short presentation covering the submitted design. This presentation leads to several lines of questioning from the panelists. Your goal is to demonstrate your skills by answering the panelist questions about your design. The moderator will remind you how much time is remaining at specific intervals. Feel comfortable moving back and forth between different parts of your presentation to answer panelist questions.

The following is an example outline for the presentation.

- Introduction, with contextual information about the project (such as business drivers and challenges)
- Key design decisions for each blueprint area
- Additional information showing alternate design options
- Reference diagrams to support answers to panelist inquiries

There is no restriction on the minimum or maximum number of slides to include. The only constraint is that you should be able to complete your presentation in 15 minutes uninterrupted. Typically, panelists jump in during the presentation to inquire about specific decisions. This is to understand your approach and potentially clarify misunderstandings within the design. Keep your answers succinct to maximize the amount of time.

There are no stipulated guidelines in the blueprint for creating a presentation. Create a structure that is comfortable for you.

Presentation tips:

1. Cover key requirements and design decisions.

2. Include any relevant artifacts so that you can refer back to them.

3. Minimize chart junk or flashy transitions. Content is king.

4. Do not include superfluous information. Talking about your entire CV and qualifications just eats up valuable time.

5. This is not a license to cram the entire design document into slide format. The presentation serves as a reference and a starting point for questioning.

Example Presentation Slides

Your slides should reflect key aspects of the project, including these:

- Key requirements, constraints, assumptions, and risks

- Topology of the infrastructure

- Logical components (storage, networking, clusters, and workloads)

- Major obstacles, problems, and risks and resolutions

Figures 5.2 through 5.5 provide examples of a design overview presentation.

Project Overview

Customers A's primary initiative was to build out a hybrid cloud solution for internal IT, leveraging local and remote resources. The existing provisioning process was fairly fluid, resulting in various side effects. Automation and orchestration of application / virtual machine life cycle was one of the key priorities.

Customer A has data center locations spread out across multiple continents.

Figure 5.2 Project overview slide example.

Requirements

R001 99.9% availability at each location

R002 Consumption-based pricing model for chargeback

R003 Service catalog user experience for end consumers

...

R0XX Instance life cycle management

Figure 5.3 Project requirements slide example.

Constraints

C001   Bandwidth between sites cannot be expanded beyond
       what is currently available

C002   Applications have latency requirements between
       client and server

...

C0XX

Figure 5.4 Constraints slide example.

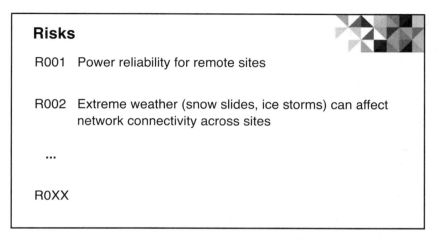

Figure 5.5 Project risks slide example.

Reference Material

Include reference slides at the end of the presentation that depict topology, connectivity, hardware components, software components, and other artifacts that will assist in responding to questions. This allows you to refer to a diagram instead of needing to whiteboard it, as demonstrated in Figure 5.6.

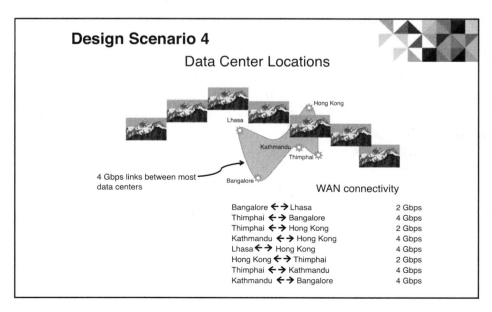

Figure 5.6 Reference material slide example.

Know Your Design

Be intimately familiar with all aspects of your design. A fully prepared candidate can white-board an entire design, if called upon. Of course, we do not expect or want candidates to do this during the defense due to time constraints.

If the design was coauthored with others, you are still responsible for understanding all aspects of the design and supporting documentation.

Understand both sides to every design consideration. Being able to address conflicts or issues is a core trait of an architect. What issues were present, and how were they addressed? What was your recommendation to the customer? How would you address or mitigate these issues today?

Referring to "best practices" alone is not sufficient. Understanding the logic behind the best practice is what counts. Best practices are specific to certain customers and use cases.

Designs often include fictional components to map more closely to the blueprint. In this case, be sure to align the fictional components with the overall requirements of the project. Seek feedback from your peers to ensure that they understand the decision points, justification, impact, and associated risk.

Entirely fictitious designs run the risk of resulting in heavily over engineered designs due to the amount of freedom available. The most over engineered design is neither exciting nor interesting, and discerning skill is difficult. To avoid this trap, leverage your peers to keep the design grounded. Requirements and constraints help shape and focus problems, providing clear challenges that lead to innovative and creative solutions.

Defense Strategy

Your goal in the defense is to showcase your skills as an architect in each domain area. Every candidate has an individual style, developed over years of experience. Having a good design on paper is not enough. Being able to explain and rationalize the design decisions made is critical. Think of it as a final presentation of design to a customer. If you lack this experience, tailored practice and high-quality feedback can make a dramatic difference.

If certain sections are not covered in the defense, it is difficult for the panelist to make an assessment. Answer the panel in a manner that demonstrates understanding and conviction of your design choices. Attempt to be as clear as possible, to help the panel separate the signal from the noise.

Listen to the panel. When they ask you to explain how you came to the design, do that—don't just explain the facts.
—Yvo Wiskere, VCDX-025

When defending the design, do not rely on "just because" or "because it's a best practice." Be prepared to explain *why* you used a best practice. You must be able to respond interactively and expand on how it relates to your design. The panelists are not attempting to induce the maximum amount of stress, but they do have to validate your understanding. Arguments are judged on how well thought-out the position is, the supporting reasoning and evidence, and how consistently the topic is argued.

Be prepared to articulate every aspect of your design. This is the most common piece of advice past defendants have provided. If you are not familiar with any particular component, put in the work to strengthen that weakness and build up the knowledge to rationalize all key design decisions.

Ask yourself, "*Why* did I make this decision?" to all your design considerations. If you cannot answer why you made it, it means you do not know your design.
—Chris Colotti, VCDX-037

Successful candidates have shown several common traits. First, they put in the effort to think through the questions that a panel was likely to pose and how to respond. Second, they studied the rubric to identify deficient areas and spent time strengthening those areas. Third, they practiced placing themselves in a defense-type situation that prepared them for the actual experience. Seek out opportunities to conduct design-type workshops to condition your mind for the actual experience.

Practice Leads to Success

Recruit peers to review your design and application package. Try to find more than one person to assist, it is beneficial to get perspective from individuals with different backgrounds and specialties. Accurate feedback is the single most powerful way to prepare yourself, improve your skills, and increase your chances of succeeding. Take any feedback or suggestion positively.

The biggest draw for the VCDX boot camps is the opportunity to participate in a defense simulation. This is a great chance to get feedback from actual panelists. The group environment is also useful for fostering discussion and ideas, especially when peers are throwing rocks at your design. Engage in deep conversations with your peers on design considerations. If you encounter a problem, force yourself to come up with a suitable explanation. You do not learn from experience itself; you learn from reflecting on experience.

Perform a dry run several months before the defense date. This gives enough buffer to make adjustments to your design and redo the practice defense. As with most academic pursuits, gaining deep understanding often requires time. Candidates are often too close to the design and are not mindful of other perspectives. Do not rush the process—this could negatively impact your confidence at the actual defense attempt.

Preparation Checklists

The following checklists provide practical reminders of important steps in the process.

Checklist: Preparation for the Defense

☐ Review all aspects of your design.

☐ Get peer review and/or feedback (mock defense, boot camp).

☐ Recognize your weaknesses, and strengthen them.

☐ Rest before the session.

☐ Arrive around 10 to 20 minutes early.

☐ If you experience anxiety, use relaxation techniques (such as deep breathing).

Checklist: Defense Overview Presentation

☐ Cover the project and important points such as requirements, constraints, assumptions, and design considerations. Include key decision points and components representing the areas identified in the blueprint:

   ☐ Requirements

   ☐ Constraints

   ☐ Assumptions

   ☐ Risks

   ☐ Availability

   ☐ Manageability

☐ Performance

☐ Recoverability

☐ Security

☐ Conceptual model

☐ Logical design

☐ Create a reference section that includes material to support your defense. This can include diagrams, tables, and other material that you plan to refer to during the defense.

☐ Rehearse your presentation, preferably in front of peers.

☐ Do *not* include extraneous information.

Checklist: Design Defense

- Preparation

  ☐ Know all areas of your design.

  ☐ Anticipate questions from the panelists.

  ☐ Identify design strengths.

  ☐ Identify design weaknesses.

- Execution

  ☐ Answer questions with concise responses.

  ☐ Refer to your presentation supporting materials section (diagrams and tables).

  ☐ Allow panelists to complete their questions before you respond.

  ☐ If you do not understand a question, ask for clarification.

  ☐ Remember that you can increase or decrease your score based on your interactions with the panelists and your responses to questions.

  ☐ Remain professional throughout (the panel is your customer).

Review

The first phase of the VCDX defense begins with the presentation and defense of the submitted panel. During 75 minutes, panelists ask questions to discern whether you can demonstrate expert-level architecture design skills. The goal is not to make your life miserable. The goal is to validate architects who can proliferate expert-level design technique worldwide.

Candidate success relies on the following factors:

1. Consulting experience

2. Technical experience

3. Panel Defense performance

All this is attainable by anyone with the proper experience, motivation, and preparation. Conducting mock defenses and peer review is the best approach to take. The point of going through the motions of a mock defense is to make the situation feel more natural. Ensure that your peers include individuals who can challenge you and throw curveballs at your design. Leverage the provided checklists to improve your level of preparedness.

Every question answered is an opportunity to demonstrate your knowledge and understanding. Keep answers relevant and concise to ensure you cover everything, but do not answer so briefly that the panelists cannot gauge understanding.

Know your design. You might have seen this stated earlier in this chapter. Many candidates fail because they simply did not consider all the options and decisions that went into their design. In most cases, this is due to a lack of preparation time. That is not to say that merely memorizing and understanding your design is sufficient enough to pass—you must be able to think on your feet, synthesize problems quickly, and embody other qualities of an architect. However, not knowing your design is such a common theme among those who fail that we must constantly reiterate it.

Chapter 6

The Design Scenario

Design is a plan for arranging elements in such a way
as best to accomplish a particular purpose.

—Charles Eames

Showcase Your Skills

What do the best architects do when faced with a design problem? How do they adapt accordingly, when provided with new information? What type of qualities do they exhibit throughout the entire process?

The second phase of the VCDX defense is the design scenario, which provides an opportunity for candidates to demonstrate their ability to gather requirements and apply them to a design. The candidate is presented with a set of design parameters and must use them to formulate a design. Here you are largely demonstrating that you know how to ask the right questions to elicit a complete set of design inputs from the customer.

Think of this exercise as a brief conversation with a customer, where you tease out requirements and supply design options. We do not expect you to complete the entire design; this is unfathomable for even the most experienced architects. You are expected to drive the conversation through all the relevant areas, per the goals of the scenario. This scenario is different from the design defense, where you primarily respond reactively to inquiries from the panelists about *your* design. As with all other phases of the defense, time management is critical to ensure that you cover the articulated design goals.

When you re-enter the room after the break, you will see two slides projected that provide contextual information for the design scenario, as shown in Figure 6.1. The moderator explains the rules and reads the design scenario aloud. Listen intently to the key points. The moment you begin asking questions, the clock starts.

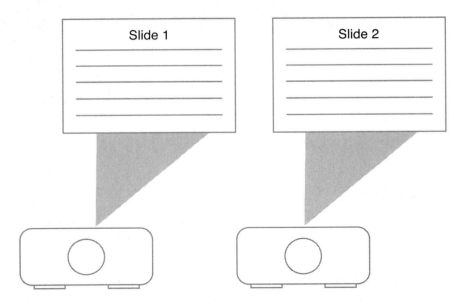

Figure 6.1   Scenario projection.

Consider these key points for the design scenario:

- You have 30 minutes for the VCDX-DCV role-play and 45 minutes for the VCDX-Cloud and VCDX-DT role-play.

- One to two contextual slides are provided.

- The candidate is the architect.

- The panelists are the customer.

Each scenario is unique, but all of them share common themes. They serve as a starting point for you to demonstrate your experience and skill set. No candidate approaches the scenario in exactly the same manner; everyone has a unique perspective on design. This small window allows the panelists to get an understanding of your thought process and design approach.

Viewing the panelists as customers sometimes throws candidates for a loop. This situation is exacerbated if the panelists happen to be composed of well-known industry personalities. It is best to put aside your knowledge of these individuals and treat the scenario as a role-play. Do not assume that your panel knows everything, even if your panel consists of well-known storage or networking experts.

> Don't be afraid to ask questions during the design and troubleshooting exercises—
> the panel members are there to help you.
> —Duncan Epping, VCDX007

The goal is to demonstrate your consultative skills to the panel. This includes articulating key points, asking relevant questions, and, most important, listening and applying responses from the panel. Use the whiteboard to form your thoughts and approach. You must address several key design objectives. As with real-world situations, not all information is shared, and information provided might be unclear, confusing, or incorrect. As the architect, you must guide the customer to the desired target state.

Do not get caught up on any minor details that can lead you down an unproductive rat hole. Successful candidates have a constant presence of mind and know where they are during each step of the design process. Scrambling at the end to cover additional areas commonly occurs, but it is seldom beneficial.

Occasionally, the conversation might shift toward a spirited technological debate. It is easy to fall into this trap, but simply state your reasoning and move on instead of expending valuable time.

Panelist's Perspective

Before the defenses, panelists review freshly created design scenarios that are specific to the defense. Some scenarios require each panelist to play a specific role; others allow for more improvisation. Ultimately, you have the responsibility of directing the conversation.

Panelists are responsible for providing the appropriate information when prompted, while evaluating your abilities. Experience is the key here. Panelists can clearly tell when someone performs this job function frequently, compared to someone who might have the technical fortitude but lacks customer-facing experience. If you are in the latter group, it's still possible to achieve success—through extensive practice. When practicing, think about how to convey your knowledge and skill set to the panelists. Having that extra bit of knowledge or insight always helps.

The panelists are keenly interested in the design methods and perspective of the candidates. Reviewing and evaluating many different designs often yields new concepts, allowing the panelists to continuously refine architectural methods for virtualization and cloud computing.

If you feel some stress or angst, this is perfectly normal. Although the panelists try their best to create a natural environment, acclimating to the situation takes time. The panel's goal is not to pose intentionally challenging questions, but to probe for information to create an assessment. They have all been through the same experience and understand if you flub a line or two. Focus on the task at hand, and the time will be over before you know it.

Design Scenario Examples

This section contains several example design scenarios that you can use for study sessions and mock defenses. Guidance is provided to spark ideas, but it is important to develop your own unique perspectives and approaches. Be creative and think about all possible solutions.

When you first see the two slides projected on the wall, you may feel overwhelmed by the amount of information. Keep in mind that not all information presented is relevant. It is your responsibility to isolate and extract key elements of the scenario. No single correct answer exists, and scenarios often change based on responses from the panelists. Stay calm, process one thing at a time, and focus on the immediate objective.

When the moderator reads the presented material, quickly internalize the key objectives and devise a plan of attack. You may find it useful to classify and prioritize key design inputs using the whiteboard to illustrate your thought process.

Design Scenario 1

Figure 6.2 shows the first slide of Design Scenario 1. Take a moment to read the provided content and think about the types of questions to ask.

Figure 6.3 shows the second slide, which provides additional contextual information, such as server count, configurations, and I/O characteristics.

Design Scenario 1

A gaming company is looking to reduce TCO and simplify management of its environment through a server consolidation project. VMware Managed Services has performed a virtualization assessment and determined that the expected consolidation ratio is 15:1 based on its target system. Due to budgetary considerations, reuse of old hardware where possible is desired.

Environment:
- NetApp Fibre Channel SAN.
- Customer has purchased 5 HP blades: 2-CPU, quad core, 2 on-board NIC ports, 2 NIC ports on 1 mezzanine card, 1 free mezzanine slot.

Objectives:
- Design cluster for two-host failure. Factor in workload balancing across resources in all phases of the project.
- Configure storage for optimal performance.
- Explain how consolidation and containment will be implemented.
- Use best practices to create a design.

Figure 6.2 Design Scenario 1, Slide 1.

Design Scenario Role-Play   **Scenario 1**   **Slide 2**

Phase	# Servers	Configuration
1	50	Two-way dual-core CPU 4 GB RAM 2 onboard NIC ports 160 GB internal disks
2	100	Two-way dual-core CPU 4 GB RAM 2 onboard NIC ports 160 GB internal disks
3	50	Two-way dual-core CPU 4 GB RAM 2 onboard NIC ports 160 GB internal disks

I/O Characteristics	# Servers
Read/Write (balanced)	90
Read Intensive	65
Write Intensive	45

Operating System	# Servers
Windows 2003	50
Windows 2008	50
Red Hat Enterprise 5	50
Windows XP	50

Figure 6.3 Design Scenario 1, Slide 2.

Candidates often fall into the trap of diving into the technical details immediately. Take a moment to look at the broader picture.

- What are the business goals for the project?
- How would you define your success criteria?
- What are the target application use cases?

Slide 1 consists largely of technical requirements, and Slide 2 contains information on the physical server specifications. Don't get too consumed with the amount of information provided on the physical specifications—extract what is necessary for your design. Use the provided capacity planner information to calculate the estimated number of target hosts. Although information about the application I/O characteristics is present, probing further into the types of applications could bring up additional information on SLAs or policies that can affect the design.

Requirements

Although this scenario explicitly declares the requirements, read between the lines to uncover additional hidden requirements. Questions to the panel can also result in newer requirements that conflict with the originally stated goal. Listen carefully and call out any discrepancies, just as you would if you were working with an actual customer. Some candidates take this a step further and begin prioritizing the various requirements.

The following requirements identified in the slides drive the discussion and design development.

R1: Reduce total cost of ownership

R2: Simplify management of environment

R3: Reuse hardware where possible

R4: Configure storage for optimal performance

R5: Explain the process of consolidation and containment

R6: Design for two-host failure, factoring in workload balancing

R7: Use best practices to create a design

Constraints

As with requirements, tease out any constraints that impact your design. The slides give very little information on the data center equipment and topology of existing systems.

Look for gaps and decide what additional information you need to gain from the panelists. Be mindful of the clock, and ration your time accordingly based on the key design objectives.

The following are identified constraints:

C1: NetApp SAN

C2: New hardware (HP blades)

C3: Existing hardware for reuse

Design Whiteboarding

If you are not comfortable diagramming and explaining concepts using the whiteboard, start practicing now. Visuals are an efficient way of conveying a message in a time-constrained exercise. Consider these suggestions to leverage the whiteboard in this exercise.

1. Initial planning

   - Methodology (topics to cover)

   - Requirements

   - Constraints

   - Information gathered from panelists

   - Scratchpad for calculations

2. Design

   - Computing

   - Networking

   - Storage

   - Dependencies

Design Methods

The most successful candidates have a standardized approach to framing questions and developing designs. When new information is presented, re-evaluate the existing design and make changes accordingly. Pay acute attention to the various perspectives, and have a keen awareness of design implications. The minutes tend to fly by quickly (ask anyone who has defended), especially if you do not manage your time properly. Have a strategy before you walk into the room.

Example Approach

1. Understand business goals and use cases.

2. Identify requirements and constraints.

3. Prioritize requirements.

    For example:

    - Design for two-host failure, factoring workload balancing.

    - Select appropriate RAID levels.

    - Explain the process of consolidation and containment.

    - Reuse hardware where possible.

4. Ask questions to clarify gaps.

5. Diagram proposed solutions (covering applicable areas, such as computing, storage, and networking).

6. Validate and adapt the proposed solution.

Design Scenario 2

Figures 6.4 and 6.5 show the slides for Design Scenario 2. Again, take a moment to read the provided content and think about the approach you will take toward creating a design.

Figure 6.5 provides additional details on server count and storage requirements.

Design Scenario 2

A multinational networking company is interested in leveraging virtualization to simplify its disaster recovery solution. The primary data center is located in San Francisco, with additional data centers in Singapore, Tokyo, and Barcelona. The first phase of the project is to virtualize a subset of the servers in the primary data center. Hardware reuse is encouraged to minimize project costs.

Environment:
- 200 physical machines (Intel and AMD)
- New hardware: Intel 2-CPU, 6-core, 32GB RAM, 2 on-board NIC ports
- Existing reusable hardware (1 Intel and 3 AMD)

Phase 1 Objectives:
- Virtualize all physical machines identified
- Support future expansion to additional sites
- Design for redundancy and flexibility to enable future growth
- Explain how consolidation and containment will be implemented

Figure 6.4 Design Scenario 2, Slide 1.

Design Scenario 2

Operating System	# Servers
Windows 2003	50
Windows 2008	50
Red Hat Enterprise 5	50
Windows XP	50

Storage Requirements	# Servers
First drive 10 GB Second drive 20 GB	50
Single drive of 50 GB	100
First drive 20 GB Second drive 20 GB	50

Figure 6.5 Design Scenario 2, Slide 2.

Let's follow the sample method outlined in the previous scenario:

1. Understand the business goals and use cases.

   "What problem are we are trying to solve?"

   Although the scenario appears to be a server consolidation project with considerations for disaster recovery, asking about business requirements and use cases might elicit information that impacts the design.

2. Identify requirements and constraints.

   Requirements:

   - R1: Support virtualization of 200 physical machines.

   - R2: Support future expansion to additional sites.

   - R3: Reuse hardware where possible.

   - R4: Design for redundancy and flexibility to enable future growth.

   - R5: Explain the process of consolidation and containment.

   Constraints:

   - C1: Mixed environment of Intel and AMD processors

   - C2: New hardware (2 CPU 6-core Intel servers, 32 GB RAM)

   - C3: Existing hardware (1 Intel and 3 AMD servers)

3. Prioritize requirements

   "If there are multiple problems, which one is the most important? How do they relate to or impact our goals?"

   While analyzing requirements, note that R2 and R4 are similar, and R1, R3, and R5 are closely linked. This comes from just a cursory glance at the provided content. Additional requirements might emerge when interacting with the panelists. As such, restate the requirements as follows:

   - Support virtualization of 200 physical machines, reusing hardware where possible.

   - Design for redundancy and flexibility for future expansion to additional sites.

   - Explain the process of consolidation and containment.

Now that you have restated and prioritized the requirements, you can begin the process of drawing out additional supporting information to formulate an initial design.

4. Ask questions to clarify gaps.

Not all the information is provided; the slides are merely a starting point. As with any customer engagements, methodically draw out the core requirements of the design. Examples:

- Are there any performance SLAs that must be maintained?
- What level of availability is required?
- What are the key workloads that will be converted?
- What is the existing networking and storage infrastructure?
- How will environments in multiple sites be managed?

5. Diagram proposed solutions (covering applicable areas such as computing, storage, and networking).

Split the whiteboard into sections, and begin diagramming proposed solutions for the scenario. Be sure to reference logical design characteristics, such as availability, manageability, performance, and security.

Computing:

- Cluster design
- Cluster features

Storage:

- Host-to-storage connectivity
- Storage features

Network:

- Virtual network design
- Physical network (if applicable)

6. Validate and adapt the proposed solution.

   You are expected to take the lead as an architect and recommend a solution, but take time to validate key decision points with the panelists. Candidates have been known to get caught up in the moment and diagram an intricate design that doesn't solve the core business issues.

> **NOTE**
>
> Occasionally take a step back to ensure that what you are proposing matches the target end state.

Design Scenario 3

Let's switch things up and look at how to design for a cloud-based scenario. Introducing cloud broadens the scope of the project, so prioritizing requirements is essential. Figures 6.6 and 6.7 provide contextual information.

Design Scenario 3

A service provider with data centers based out of Denver, CO, is looking to enter the emerging cloud marketplace. Internal research on cloud computing has been conducted, leading to the creation of a solution definition and roadmap.

The customer has existing virtual and physical environments and would like to reuse as much equipment as possible for the initial phase. Because the customer is a service provider, the design must be scalable while also cost-effective.

Security of the environment is paramount because target customers have varying compliance regulations. Multiple connectivity options should be provided to support end user application use cases.

Figure 6.6   Cloud Design Scenario, Slide 1.

Design Scenario 3

Environment Details:
- Computing: Mix of Cisco blades and white-box server systems
- Networking:
  - Predominantly Cisco networking gear, with several F5 load balancers
  - 1 GB to 10 GB connectivity available
  - IDS/IPS physical devices
- Storage:
  - Variety of storage options with SAN, NFS, and ISCSI systems
  - Separate isolated storage network
  - 10 TB of storage available

Task: Design a solution that meets customer requirements.

Figure 6.7 Cloud Design Scenario, Slide 2.

Cloud requires additional components on top of virtualization to automate and orchestrate business processes. Although managing the amount of complexity introduced into the environment to achieve cloud capabilities is a persistent design goal, the method devised in the previous scenarios is still applicable.

1. Understand the business goals and use cases.

   The primary business goal is to gain a foothold in the cloud computing marketplace through the creation of cloud services. The service provider wants to update its brand as a next-generation cloud computing service provider.

   Initially, there are two offerings, a container-based offering and a pay-as-you-go offering. Each offering comes in a variety of sizes, as specified in the service definition.

2. Identify requirements and constraints.

   Ask specific questions about the project requirements and constraints, to gather more information for your design. This scenario differs slightly from the previous two, in that the slides do not state the explicit requirements. Consider these examples of requirements that can emerge by asking questions on the necessary cloud capabilities.

- Requirements:

    - R1: The system can scale to 5,000 virtual machines (scalability).

    - R2: An API is exposed for end users (integration).

    - R3: Metering is required for accurate billing (chargeback).

    - R4: End users can self-provision applications from a catalog (self-service).

    - R5: The solution must provide 99.9% availability (availability).

    - R6: Tenant data and applications must be isolated (multitenancy).

    - R7: The system must address the virtual machine life cycle (service life cycle).

    - R8: Efficiency of hardware must be addressed, to improve profit margins (resource pooling).

- Constraints:

    - C1: Existing hardware must be used for the first phase.

    - C2: A limited number of VLANs is available.

    - C3: The budget must include resources for training administrators.

    - C4: Legacy management and billing systems must be used.

    - C5: 10 TB of storage is available.

3. Prioritize requirements.

    In this case, the requirements are fairly distinct. Work with the customer to prioritize the requirements and understand the mapping to technology. The final result might look something like this:

    - R1: Provide 99.9% availability.

    - R2: Isolate tenant data and applications.

    - R3: Expose an API for end users.

    - R4: Ensure that the system can scale to 5,000 virtual machines.

    - R5: Ensure efficiency of hardware, to improve profit margins.

    - R6: Address the virtual machine life cycle.

- R7: Use metering, for accurate billing.

- R8: Enable end users to self-provision applications from a catalog.

4. Ask questions to clarify gaps.

Further questioning is needed to understand how to design various components of the cloud.

Examples:

- Please elaborate on the security and compliance requirements. Which compliance regulations need to be supported?

- Based on the service definition, what types of Service Level Agreements (SLAs) will be maintained with the tenants?

- What types of catalog items are required? Base operating systems? Complete applications?

- Is it acceptable to provide isolation through the use of overlay network technology? Can the network infrastructure support this today?

- What are the eventual goals for the cloud-management system and multiple data center locations?

You might eventually get into details such as Virtual eXtensible LAN (VXLAN), storage profiles, virtual data center, single sign-on (SSO), and API extensions. If these topics exist in the design, display your understanding of them as they relate to core design choices. For example, VXLAN provides Layer 2 over Layer 3 capabilities, but it necessitates configuring multicast and increasing the maximum transmission unit (MTU) for endpoints participating in the VXLAN transport VLAN.

The Art of Explanations

Be able to articulate the rationale behind any statement that you make. Sometimes panelists appear to act like inquisitive two-year-olds to validate true depth of understanding. The key is to provide very succinct explanations that clearly articulate the reasoning behind a certain design decision. If you cannot answer the "Why?" question, research the topic until you can back up the statement with utmost confidence. Ponder what you are trying to convey to the panelists, and what the clearest explanation would be.

Statement: "Start out with allocation pool virtual data centers and pay-as-you-go."

Why?

Answer: "Based on your cost constraints and service offering models, this gives you the capability to control overcommitment and provides flexibility for end users."

How?

Answer: "Allocation pool virtual data centers provide the capability to set guarantees or reservations on the container, and pay-as-you-go allows deployment of resources up until a specified limit."

An easy way to avoid this line of questioning is to preemptively provide succinct explanations for design choices.

Diagram proposed solutions (covering applicable areas: computing, storage, networking, and so on).

Split the whiteboard into sections, and begin diagramming proposed solutions for the scenario. Be sure to reference logical design characteristics such as availability, manageability, performance, and security.

Figures 6.8 through 6.10 show examples of design artifacts.

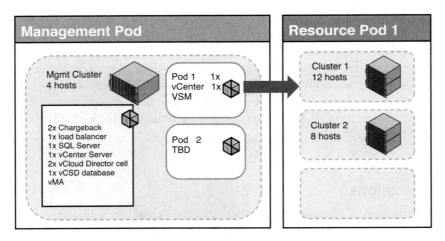

Figure 6.8 Cloud pod design, a cluster diagram showing separation of management and cloud resource group functions.

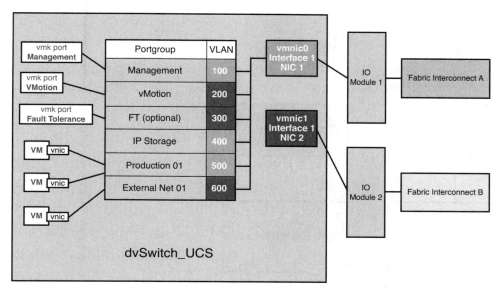

Figure 6.9 Network design, illustrating the virtual switch to physical networking component mapping and how traffic types are isolated.

Validate and adapt the proposed solution.

Because of the complexity of cloud solutions, remaining organized and methodical throughout the process is vital. The number of components involved increases the importance of traceability. As the architect, be relentless in managing the requirements and mapping them to design decisions. In addition, time management is more challenging, especially when trying to determine how deep to go in each area.

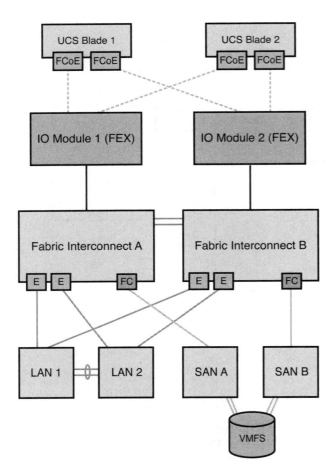

Figure 6.10   UCS connectivity. Host-to-storage layout for the blade server system.

Design Scenario 4

Figure 6.11 is a desktop-based scenario. The approach used should not be radically different, although the desktop focus has specific implications on design areas such as performance and security.

Design Scenario 4

A multinational energy drink company is seeking a unified virtual desktop solution for its field and remote teams. The goal is to host all user data centrally in the two primary data centers and allow users to access their desktops from anywhere. Because this is the pilot project for a potentially larger rollout, the end user experience with respect to performance is critical. Depending on the business unit, some users are more sensitive to latency than others.

  Primary requirements:
  - Scalable up to 1,000+ users with 250 concurrent connections
  - Multifactor authentication into desktop environment
  - Secure virtual desktop environment for end users
  - Consistent end user experience especially for power users
  - Meet existing availability SLAs
  - Provide roadmap for data center failover

Objective: Create a virtual desktop solution that meets the customer requirements.

Figure 6.11   Desktop Scenario, Slide 1.

Figure 6.12 provides specific desktop statistics from an earlier analysis.

Use the process outlined in the previous examples to work through this desktop design scenario. We leave the details as an exercise for the reader.

Design Scenario 4

Performance Analysis Summary:

Start Date: Oct 1, 2012

End Date: Oct 30, 2012

Desktops evaluated: 457

Users evaluated: 851

Average IOPS for all desktops: **5.72 IOPS**

VDI UX, All Machines	Count
Good	423
Fair	23
Poor	1

Peak Resource Consumers

Name	Peak Login Delay	Avg CPU Queue	Peak CPU Queue	Avg Mem Used	Peak Mem Used	Peak Swap Used	Avg Disk IOPS	Peak Disk IOPS	Lowest VDI UX
sparc	101.00s	4.27	52.00	701 MB	732 MB	1.0 GB	7.6	15	2.3
room18	42.00s	1.49	9.00	623 MB	761 MB	678 MB	3.23	69	2.5
den101	33.00s	3.30	11.00	1.02 GB	1.11 GB	1.2 GB	6.7	93	2.6
dn_yuzu	n/a	0.82	9.00	325 MB	1.3 MB	720 MB	5.42	45	2.6
tu1995	10.00s	1.93	8.00	1.00 GB	2.10 GB	1.71 GB	4.03	50	2.7
ICE_mnst	10.00s	2.27	6.00	732 MB	963 MB	612 MB	3.22	67	2.7

Figure 6.12   Desktop Scenario, Slide 2.

Review

The design scenario is a role-play of an architect meeting with a customer. The VCDX-DCV is 30 minutes; the VCDX-Cloud and VCDX-DT are 45 minutes in length. Two contextual slides are presented as a starting set of design parameters. You are the architect, and the panelists represent the customer.

During the defense, you must think aloud, interact with the panelists, and use the whiteboard to demonstrate your design approach. Consider the five phases for developing an architecture specific to a customer. Categorizing and prioritizing design inputs at the onset helps narrow the focus and clarify additional required information.

Use an approach that demonstrates the methodology you use. We provided the following as one possible approach as a checklist. Modify and adapt this accordingly.

- ☐ Understand the business goals and use cases.
- ☐ Identify requirements and constraints.

☐ Prioritize requirements.

☐ Ask questions to clarify gaps.

☐ Diagram proposed solutions.

☐ Validate and adapt proposed solutions.

Successful candidates demonstrate several common traits. First, they put in the effort to think through the questions that a panel was likely to pose and how to respond. Second, they studied the rubric to identify deficient areas and spend time strengthening those areas. Third, they practiced placing themselves in a defense-type situation that prepared them for the actual experience. Seek out opportunities to conduct design-type workshops to condition your mind for the actual experience.

Consider these closing tips:

- **Think aloud:** Contrary to popular belief, panelists cannot read your mind. A pause here and there is fine to gather your thoughts, but an extended pause makes us wonder whether you are thinking about dinner plans. Not articulating your thought process means fewer data points from the panel. When you encounter an unknown, think aloud.

- **Focus on panelist interaction:** Drive the conversation using a logical approach. Asking precise questions saves time by reducing the need for follow-up questions. Never assume that the panelists understand the underlying intent of the question. Be aware of all interactions with the panel, and ensure that the solution aligns with the business problems.

- **Practice:** Knowing something and being able to articulate it are two separate things. Deliberate practice and high-quality feedback help increase the signal-to-noise ratio.

- **Relax:** If you start to feel nervous, take a deep breath. Panelists will not ask you to do quantum mechanics or perform complex integrals.

Candidates often comment on how quickly time seems to elapse, especially if you get into a good flow. It bears repeating: Be organized and manage your time well. Think of the exercise as a dialogue among architects, and the experience might actually be enjoyable.

Chapter 7

The Troubleshooting Scenario

There are no big problems;
there are just a lot of little problems.

—Henry Ford

The Troubleshooting Scenario demonstrates a candidate's ability to troubleshoot between a design issue and an implementation or operational issue. VCDX-DCV is 15 minutes in length, and the VCDX-Cloud and VCDX-DT are 30 minutes in length. Several contextual slides are provided as a starting point. The goal is to demonstrate your ability to work through a problem in a methodical and logical manner. The problem could be design, build, or operations related.

There is no break between the design scenario and the troubleshooting scenario. Once the slides are projected, the moderator reads both slides aloud. You'll have a few minutes to digest the information before the timer is started. The format and guidelines are very similar to the design scenario. The panelist acts as the customer, and you have the ability to ask them to perform actions on the environment or lookup information on the Internet.

Conducting the Troubleshooting Scenario

Troubleshooting scenarios include many options and red herrings, similar to a murder mystery game. This allows the panelists to assess your analytical skills and decision-making process.

Thinking Aloud

In the troubleshooting scenarios, consider the solution architecture and implementation as you work on the root cause. Provide guidance on your approach to resolution. Inspect design decisions, implementation decisions, and the methods for gaining evidence (logs, approach to resolution, and use of commands). Your approach and understanding is more important than finding the root cause. Throughout the scenario, clearly showing your thought process improves your chances of a better score.

Asking Questions

Work methodically, and ask questions relevant to the problematic area. For example, if the presented symptom suggests network-related issues, ask questions about the logical and physical network design. However, this might not be the culprit. Listen to the panelists' responses to eliminate one area at a time. Apply what you have discovered back to the troubleshooting scenario. Asking questions without making any connections is a fruitless exercise.

When looking at the preponderance of evidence, contemplate what is more probable. What are the chances that I'm on the right track? How does everything fit together?

Do not jump to conclusions or quickly answer, even if you are certain of the solution. This limits the opportunity to demonstrate your process of methodically troubleshooting a problem.

Using a Whiteboard or Paper

Use the whiteboard to record the answers to your questions, as well as any information presented to you on the troubleshooting slides. Draw any logical or physical diagrams relevant to the design. Illustrate what you are thinking and explain verbally the "what" and "why."

Troubleshooting Analysis

As a starting point, not all information is provided. In addition, as in the real world, the scenario includes potentially conflicting information.

Example: Conflicting Information

- Trouble Report Item 1:

  The storage administrator states that nothing was changed around the time the problem started.

- Trouble Report Item 2:

  All ESXi hosts experienced loss of access to the same LUNs on a storage array.

- Analysis:

  - You must determine how to address the conflict, provide justification, and demonstrate analysis skills to resolve conflicts.

  - Ask the storage administrator whether any SAN events occurred around the time the problem began and ask for an explanation of what would have caused the outage. If the SAN admin still insists that nothing happened, ask for the ESXi logs (such as vmkernel/vmkernel.log) and look for SAN-related messages indicating loss of connectivity or failover events from all affected hosts.

Requirements Analysis

What are you trying to solve? What other information can you get? What constraints, assumptions, and risks are you working with to help with troubleshooting?

The Panelist Perspective

The panelists are looking for skills in evaluating a problem, determining whether it is design or implementation related, and deciding on the path needed for resolution.

A methodical approach is best. Based on the scenario presented, provide the target areas to pursue initially. The panelists will compare your approach against alternate paths that you could have taken to resolve the problem.

The panelists will focus on identifying your approach and how you adjust when a path taken does not work out.

Example Scenarios

For the following examples, we provide guidance on one approach for each scenario. The steps provided are a subset of what would occur in a full scenario in a panel defense session. They do not include all the steps required for achieving passing scores, so use them as a learning aid.

These examples provide two slides for each scenario. Some sample interactions between the candidate and the panelists are shown. Notes on the approach successful candidates take are provided as well.

Example Troubleshooting Scenario #1

You will be presented with one or more slides that cover the scenario information. Some information might be presented in response to your questions to the panelists. Figure 7.1 represents the first slide.

Troubleshooting Scenario Role-Play   **Scenario 1**   **Slide 1**

You have been asked to troubleshoot a recently built vSphere proof-of-concept environment for a customer.

Reported Issues:
- The Microsoft Windows 2008 (64-bit) virtual machines on this particular ESX Server are hanging over a period of time.
- Some user groups report loss of access to key applications.
- Access to the host will sometimes be nonresponsive when connecting with a PuTTY SSH client.
- Virtual machines are experiencing sporadic slowness.

Configuration Details
- 100 virtual machines running on 5 ESX hosts (2 quad-core 2 GHz CPU, 64 GB RAM).
- The virtual machine's files are stored on a single LUN shared between hosts with a mixture of VMFs and RDM placement.
- 10 GB backbone network; ESX hosts are redundantly connected to the production network.

Accompanying slide shows high-level diagram of the networking and storage layout.

Figure 7.1   Troubleshooting Scenario Role-Play: Scenario 1, Slide 1

Figure 7.2 shows a second slide with additional information.

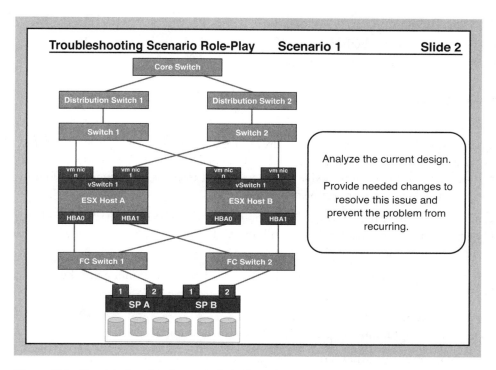

Figure 7.2 Troubleshooting Scenario Role-Play: Scenario 1, Slide 2.

Analysis of Existing Information

Analyze existing information by identifying validated facts, possible solution areas, and questionable details.

Validated Facts

- Applications not accessible are in virtual machines on the affected host.
- The host is not accessible via SSH/PuTTY.

Solution Areas

The diagram shows both network and SAN connectivity. Rule out one of them by asking further questions.

Questionable Details

The slide does not specify whether the problem is network or storage related. Rule out each section at a time by asking relevant questions.

Asking Questions

1. Has a support ticket been opened?

2. Can the host be accessed via DCUI (Direct Connect UI) either physically at the host or via a remote management board (such as ILO or DRAC)? This should rule out management network connectivity. If the host is not responsive even via DCUI, it is not a management network problem.

3. Can you ping the virtual machine? This should rule out the virtual machine network. However, it might not be conclusive—a hung VM might not respond even when there is no network problem.

4. Are other hosts experiencing this problem? If so, what is in common with these hosts?

5. If you rule out the network, get more details on the storage. Look more closely at the connectivity diagram for any inconsistencies with best practices.

6. What type of storage array is this (active/active or active/passive, ALUA)?

7. Ask the SAN admins whether any SAN events have occurred, and request that they look through the storage array logs.

Whiteboarding

Write key points on the whiteboard. Use the answers to your questions to write down what they mean and how they affect your decision path and conclusions.

Write down the areas you want to cover and verbally explain why.

Draw out alternative connections. If you see any incorrect connectivity, draw what you propose to correct it.

Methodical Approach

As outlined earlier, identify the possible problem areas. In this example, it could be VMs, hosts, or infrastructure. Eliminate each area using the answers to your questions.

You are not expected to be an expert on each component outside of vSphere—ask questions to become familiar with these external factors.

It is always advisable to request logs, as long as you know which events you need to look for. Don't just say, "Are there any errors in the logs?" The best approach is to identify the logs and type of errors. For example, you might ask, "Are there any path failover events in the vmkernel/vmkernel.log files?" or "Are there any SCSI sense codes?" If you find any, you could ask the panel to look up what they mean.

After you zone in on the possible problem area, ask more detailed questions.

In this example, the array is active/passive, and you identify that the cabling does not meet best practices because each fabric is connected to one Storage Processor (SP) instead of both. This would be something to rule out. This could cause a path thrashing state. Look for events that indicate one or more LUNs flapping between SPs. Are the symptoms consistent with such a state?

It is possible that Host A lost SAN connectivity on HBA1, and then later Host B lost connectivity to the SAN on HBA0. This leaves Host A with access to SP A only and *Host B* with access to SP B only. As a result, each of them requests the array to transfer ownership of the LUNs to the SP to which they have access. This results in the same condition of the LUNs bouncing between SPs.

Figure 7.3 shows how connectivity failures can lead to path thrashing.

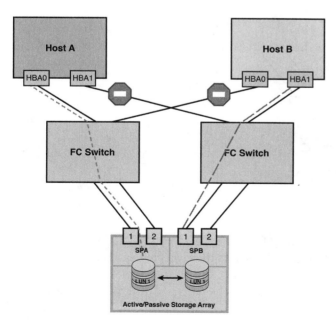

Figure 7.3 Path thrashing from connectivity failure.

If you confirm that this is the root cause, request that the cabling connectivity be changed, and clearly state the necessary changes. For example, change the Fibre Channel (FC) Switch 1 connection from SP A, Port 2 to SP B, Port 2; and change FC switch 2's connection from SP B, Port 2 to SP A, Port 2.

Another possibility is that the vSphere admin decides to load-balance the I/O over the SPs by changing the default preferred storage path (PSP) from VMW_PSP_MRU to VMW_PSP_FIXED and then sets the preferred path to some LUNs via HBA 0 and others via HBA 1 on Host A, but accidentally sets the reverse on Host B. This would result in the same condition, even without connectivity failure.

Figure 7.4 shows how the wrong PSP can lead to path thrashing.

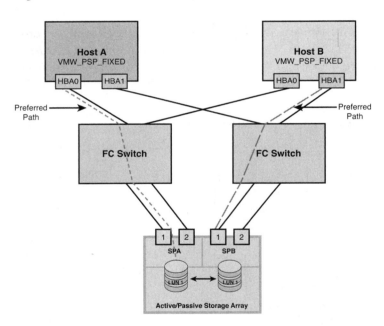

Figure 7.4   Path thrashing from an incorrect PSP choice.

If this is the root cause, change the default PSP back to VMW_PSP_MRU and connect each FC switch to a port on each SP. Figure 7.5 shows the corrected design.

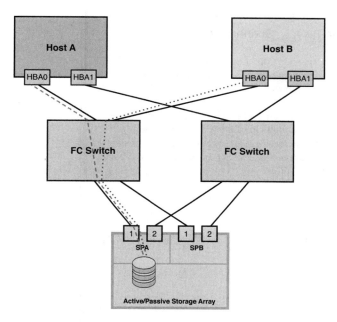

Figure 7.5 Corrected SAN design to resolve the path thrashing.

Does this alleviate the problem?

Example Troubleshooting Scenario #2

You are presented with one or more slides that cover the scenario information. Some information might be presented in response to your questions to the panelists. Figure 7.6 represents the first slide.

Figure 7.7 shows a second slide with additional information.

Troubleshooting Scenario Role-Play   Scenario 2   Slide 1

A financial organization adopted virtualization in 2005 and is currently 80% virtualized. The primary virtualization administrator has gone on vacation, and the rest of the team is not familiar with the environment.

Recently, access to the vCenter Server has become intermittent and, in some cases, inaccessible altogether. Failed connection attempts to vCenter occur from other management tools and some clients. The last action taken by the administrator was to add the backup network because we realized the local SQL instance was not being backed up.

Identify the root cause and mitigation options. Provide the security team with appropriate justification of the issue.

The security team is requesting a full analysis of why the vCenter Server has become unresponsive.

Figure 7.6   Troubleshooting Scenario Role-Play: Scenario 2, Slide 1.

Troubleshooting Scenario Role-Play			Scenario 2		Slide 2
Host	IP Address	Netmask	Gateway	VLAN	vSwitch
vc1.corp.local	192.168.130.120 192.168.100.120	255.255.255.0 255.255.255.0	192.168.130.10	130 100	dvs_prod dvs_backup
ad1.corp.local	192.168.130.110	255.255.255.0	192.168.130.10	130	dvs_prod
vcb.corp.local	192.168.130.130 192.168.100.130	255.255.255.0 255.255.255.0	192.168.130.10	130 100	Physical
netbkup.corp.local	192.168.130.112 192.168.100.112	255.255.255.0 255.255.255.0	192.168.130.10	130 100	Physical
esx01.corp.local	192.168.140.150	255.255.255.0	192.168.140.10	140	Physical
esx02.corp.local	192.168.140.151	255.255.255.0	192.168.140.10	140	Physical

Figure 7.7   Troubleshooting Scenario Role-Play: Scenario 2, Slide 2.

Analysis of Existing Information

To analyze existing information, identify validated facts, possible solution areas, and questionable details.

Validated Facts

Analyze existing information by identifying validated facts, possible solution areas, and questionable details.

1. The last change done before the problem was reported was that the administrator added a backup network.

2. Access to vCenter Server is intermittent over the network.

3. Attempts to access vCenter Server via management tools and other clients failed.

4. The backup network was added to back up the local SQL server.

Solution Areas

The following are possible solution areas:

1. Network configuration problems

2. Storage configuration problems

Questionable Details

- It is not clear what "local SQL server" means.

- It is not clear which management tools or clients are used.

Asking Questions

First, verify the nature of the problem:

1. Which "management tools" or clients are used to access the VMware vCenter Server?

2. Which version of vCenter Server and ESXi is used?

3. Is vCenter Server protected with VMware HA or other availability configuration?

4. What do you mean by "SQL server installed locally"?

Now rule out resource contention problems:

1. What is the CPU and memory utilization on the host on which vCenter is running?

2. Is VMware DRS enabled? If so, is vCenter Server vMotioned to other hosts?

3. If not, can you manually vMotion vCenter to another host?

Then rule out a storage issue:

1. What storage array is used?

2. What is the default PSP?

Rule out network issues:

1. Can you ping vCenter Server's IP address/FQDN from a physical machine?

2. Can you ping vCenter Server's IP address/FQDN from a virtual machine on the same host?

3. Can you ping vCenter Server's IP address/FQDN from a virtual machine on another host?

4. Can you access vCenter Server via remote console? If so, can you ping out to the network?

5. What exact changes were done to add the "backup network"?

6. From the IP list, I see that vDS is used. What type of physical switch is used?

Whiteboarding

Draw the virtual network configuration, including the vDS port groups and related configurations that you obtain from the panelists.

Methodical Approach

The first set of questions clarifies the nature of the problem. Is the virtual machine not responsive, or is it running but not reachable over the network?

The second set of questions rules out performance-related issues. If the problem continues after vMotioning the virtual machine to another host with enough resources, it is not resource related.

Asking for storage information could rule out storage-related issues such as I/O contention or path thrashing. In this case, storage might not be the issue.

Now move on to the network troubleshooting: Pinging by IP address always works, but using FQDN works intermittently. This could indicate a DNS round-robin issue.

If so, ask about the DNS configuration. If the IP address is registered via dynamic DNS, check the latest IP address added via the backup network configuration and how it was configured.

Example Troubleshooting Scenario #3

You are presented with one or more slides that cover the scenario information. Some information could be presented in response to your questions to the panelists. Figure 7.8 represents the first slide.

Figure 7.9 shows a second slide with additional information.

Troubleshooting Scenario Role-Play   Scenario 3   Slide 1

A large corporation is implementing a VDI (Virtual Desktop Infrastructure) based on VMware View 5.0. It has not gone live yet with this environment because its tests uncovered severe performance problems.

You have been chosen by this corporation to evaluate the current design.

Your task is to identify the root cause and provide any design changes you see necessary to resolve the problem.

Figure 7.8   Troubleshooting Scenario Role-Play: Scenario 3, Slide 1.

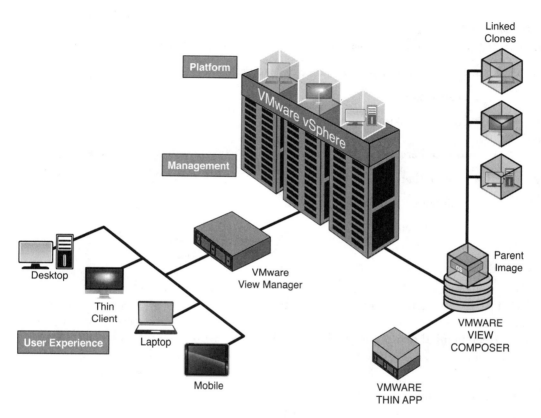

Figure 7.9 Troubleshooting Scenario Role-Play: Scenario 3, Slide 2

Analysis of Existing Information

Analyze existing information by identifying validated facts, possible solution areas, and questionable details.

Validated Facts

Based solely on the content of the slides, not much information is provided. All you know is that it is a View 5.0 environment and that the main symptom of the problem is "severe performance problem." Because this is not a design you provided, you should be allowed to request the original design. The second slide presents a high-level version.

Solution Areas

In a View 5.0 environment, performance issues can arise in one or more of these areas:

1. View client (aka thin client) connectivity to the View Manager.

   - Networking

   - Remote desktop protocols

2. VMware vSphere environment on which the virtual desktops are running.

   - Computing

   - Storage

   - Linked clones

Questionable Details

The problem description is a somewhat vague "severe performance problem." You need to get some metrics that were used to quantify the performance and determine whether it is based on user perception doing their daily tasks or their experience on physical desktops. Keep in mind that this is the first time this organization is using a VMware View environment.

Asking Questions

First identify the exact nature of the problem:

1. Did you submit a support ticket with VMware? If so, ask for the information provided and any suggestions made by the VMware Support Engineer.

2. Which tests did you run to measure the performance? Which data did you use as a baseline?

3. Does this happen all the time? If not, is there a pattern?

Now start asking questions about the infrastructure.

- Client-side questions:

  - What type of thin client are you using? Is it on the VMware HCL?

  - Which protocols does the thin client use?

  - What is the type and speed of network connecting to the View Manager?

- vSphere infrastructure questions:

  Ask questions about the cluster architecture:

  - What is the make and model of each ESXi server in the cluster?

  - What is the type, speed, and count of CPUs/host, as well as the RAM size?

  - Which version of ESXi and vCenter Server is used?

  Network questions:

  - What is the number and type of NICs per host, including the configured speed?

  - What types of virtual switches are being used?

  - What is the NIC teaming failover policy?

  Storage questions:

  - What is the storage array make and model?

  - What is the storage connectivity and protocol (FC, FCoE, iSCSI, or NFS)?

  - Which VMFS version is in use? If it is VMFS5, was it freshly created or upgraded from an earlier version?

  - How are the LUNs provisioned (thin or thick)?

  View Composer questions:

  - How many parent images are used for the same desktop type and operating system?

  - What are the details of linked clones and their placement on the data stores?

  - Is storage DRS in use?

Whiteboarding

As you get answers to questions for a solution area, draw or build tables with the answers. Again, be sure to note all responses you get from the panelists.

Methodical Approach

Cover each of the solution areas, and focus on the most likely root cause.

Walk your way through the design, starting with the client access. To rule that out, ask to use one of the desktops directly via vSphere Client's Remote Console. If there is no improvement, move on to the infrastructure. Rule out the compute resources by using a smaller number of desktops, reducing quantity until you are down to a single desktop.

If the problem still exists with a single desktop, you need to focus on the linked clone details. If all desktops share the same parent image, the problem should not exist if you use a single virtual machine because there would be no contention for the storage or network resources.

Even though the problem exists with a single running desktop, it could be a result of storage resource contention. A possibility is guest OS file system alignment with the underlying physical storage. Check the VMware Knowledgebase for known issues related to file system alignment.

It is permissible to ask the panel to look up any information on the web, such as VMware Knowledge Base (KB) articles.

It is a known fact that, on ESXi 5, the linked clone files are created at a certain granularity size, the size by which the linked clone files are grown. This can result in a file system misalignment even if the parent image's virtual disks are correctly aligned.

Consider upgrading to vSphere 5.1 and the View release, which takes advantage of space efficient sparse disks (SE sparse disks), which grow in a configurable grain size. Check with the storage vendor about the recommended grain size, for better alignment.

Example Troubleshooting Scenario #4

You are presented with one or more slides that cover the scenario information. Some information might be presented in response to your questions to the panelists. Figure 7.10 represents the first slide.

Figure 7.11 shows a second slide with additional information.

Troubleshooting Scenario Role-Play   Scenario 4   Slide 1

You have been asked to troubleshoot a vCloud Director 5.1 environment. The vCloud architects and adminstrators have utilized the vCloyd Architecture Toolkit (vCAT) for both design and operational reference.

The security team reported that some VMs have lost access to the public network. These VMs are critical for operations and security management.

The current vCloud deployment consists of vCloud Director 5.1, vSphere 5.1, vCenter Orchestrator, vCenter Chargeback, vCloud Network and Security product suite, and other related technologies.

Both standard and distributed vSwitchs exist in this environment.

Figure 7.10 Troubleshooting Scenario Role-Play: Scenario 4, Slide 1.

Troubleshooting Scenario Role-Play   **Scenario 4**   **Slide 2**

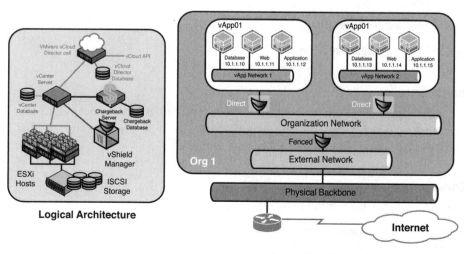

Figure 7.11 Troubleshooting Scenario Role-Play: Scenario 4, Slide 2.

Analysis of Existing Information

Analyze existing information by identifying validated facts, possible solution areas, and questionable details.

Validated Facts

Based solely on the content of the slides, all you know is that it is a vCloud Director 5.1 environment and that the main symptom of the problem is "Some VMs lost access to public network." Because this is not a design you provided, you should be allowed to ask to see the original design. The second slide presents a high-level version.

Solution Areas

In a vCloud 5.1 environment, VM network connectivity can be in one or more of these areas:

1. Network connectivity
   a. vSwitch uplinks
   b. Physical switch connectivity
   c. NIC teaming policy
   d. vSwitch port groups

2. vShield
   a. vShield Manager
   b. vShield Edge Appliances
   c. VXLAN configuration

Questionable Details

The problem description is a somewhat general "virtual machines lost connectivity." Get some clarification on which virtual machines have experienced this problem and whether they are on the same host.

Asking Questions

First, identify the exact nature of the problem:

1. Did you submit a support ticket with VMware? If so, ask for the information provided and any suggestions made by the VMware Support Engineer.

2. Which virtual machines experienced loss of public network connectivity?

3. Are these virtual machines on the same host?

Now start asking questions about the infrastructure.

- Network design and connectivity:

    - What types of vSwitches are in use (standard, distributed)?

    - How are these switches connected to the physical switches?

    - What is the NIC teaming configuration?

    - If the affected virtual machines are on the same host, are any links down? Was there a NIC failover?

    - Can you access the virtual machines via Virtual Machine Remote Console (VMRC)?

    - Can you access the virtual machines via Remote Desktop Protocol (RDP), if configured?

- vShield questions:

    - Are you able to access vShield Manager?

    - If so, are the vShield Edge virtual appliances running?

    - If you find one that is not running, can this be the root cause?

Whiteboarding

As you receive answers to your questions, draw or build tables with the answers. Again, be sure to note all responses you get from the panelists.

Methodical Approach

First, troubleshoot this as a standard network problem. If you rule out physical and virtual switch problems, review the vCloud networking design. vShield Edge appliances control access to external networks. Virtual machines protected by vShield appliances lose connectivity when the corresponding appliance is down.

If this is the case, explain that HA clusters should have detected that the appliance was down and restarted it. However, because the vShield appliances do not have Virtual Machine tools available, Guest OS monitoring is not possible.

NOTE

Do not fall prey to "diagnosis momentum." Fixating on the first issue you find tends to blind you from the bigger picture or alternate solutions. Don't stop searching once you discover a problem. If the answer appears too obvious, take a step back and ponder what else could be wrong.

Review

The VCDX Troubleshooting Scenario is a role-play that is 15 minutes for the VCDX-DCV program and 30 minutes for the VCDX-Cloud and VCDX-DT. You act as the architect, and the panelists act as a customer. Additional slides might be available if "trigger" questions are raised, such as, "May I see the Blue Screen of Death (BSoD) display?"

This chapter covered design troubleshooting scenarios. The intention is for you to troubleshoot the design rather than a specific technical problem. Most, if not all, designs presented will appear to test your technical troubleshooting skills. However, don't be intimidated—just analyze the design elements that could be the possible source of the problem.

Make sure you are methodical in your approach, and write down all responses you get from the panel. Think on your feet and use the whiteboard. Think aloud and let the panel know your thought process. Rest assured that even if you do not solve the problem, the panel looks at the journey rather than the destination. Remember to think aloud. If the panelists cannot hear your thoughts, it is exceedingly difficult to analyze your thought process.

Explain what you are convinced of and what needs clarification. Consider all aspects of the scenario, rather than rapidly firing out possible answers. Many candidates tend to stop probing after finding a major issue, but this natural cognitive tendency risks missing details that lead to a larger systematic issue.

Conclusion

This concludes the VCDX Defense.

—[VCDX Moderator]

The intrigue. The drama. The suspense. Hours toiled away. All this becomes worthwhile the moment you peer into your overcrowded email inbox and read:

```
"Congratulations! You have achieved the VMware Certified Design Expert..."
```

A bolt of energy ripples through you as if you'd just stuck a fork into an electric socket. Followed by a round of whooping and screaming that might prompt your neighbor to call the police.

Whether you are an experienced architect or a newcomer to the data center, we hope that the insights provided have been beneficial. Achieving VCDX is a game changer, an immediate shot of credibility that follows you throughout your career. Barring that, you'll have a unique number that you can monogram into your shirts or put on a vanity plate.

Here are some parting tips:

- Write down specific objectives and set firm deadlines.
- Break up activities and tasks into chunks. This keeps you from biting off too much at once.
- Look at potential projects and consider the tangible outputs
- Execute the design projects and harvest the IP

- Associate with others striving for the same goal and share knowledge
- Reflect on your own design perspective and experience
- Challenge yourself by trying things you don't know how to do
- Make it fun; this helps the process become much more tolerable
- Never stop learning and asking questions

A final quote from Lucius Annaeus Seneca, a Roman Philosopher:

> "It's not because things are difficult that we dare not venture. It's because we dare not venture that they are difficult."

References

Books and Links

Arrasjid, Epping, and Kaplan. *Foundations for Cloud Computing with VMware vSphere 4*. United States: USENIX Association, 2010.

Arrasjid, Lin, Veeramraju, Kaplan, Epping, and Haines. *Cloud Computing with VMware vCloud Director*. United States: USENIX Association, 2011.

Khalil. *Storage Implementation in vSphere 5.0, Technology Deep Dive*. VMware Press, 2012.

The Open Group, *TOGAF® Version 9.1*, Online, 2011. See http://pubs.opengroup.org/architecture/togaf9-doc/arch/

Tufte. *Envisioning Information*. United States: Graphics Press, 1990.

VMware vCAT Team. *VMware vCloud Architecture Toolkit (vCAT), Technical and Operational Guidance for Cloud Success*. VMware Press, 2013.

VMware vCAT Team. VMware vCloud Architecture Toolkit (vCAT). Document Center electronic release, 2012. See http://www.vmware.com/go/vcat.

Zachman. *Conceptual, Logical, Physical: It Is Simple*. Online, 2000–2011. See http://www.zachman.com/ea-articles-reference/58-conceptual-logical-physical-it-is-simple-by-john-a-zachman.

Training Courses

VMware and partners offer multiple training programs that relate to achieving the VCDX certification. Visit http://www.vmware.com/go/vcdx for more details.

Glossary

VCA VMware Certified Associate.

VCA-DT VMware Certified Associate–Desktop. This is the associate-level category in the VMware certification path for desktop.

VCAP VMware Certified Advanced Professional is at the middle, or advanced professional category, in the VMware certification path. VCAP certification exists for the areas of data center virtualization (VCAP-DCA, VCAP-DCD), desktop (VCAP-DTA, VCAP-DTD), and cloud (VCAP-CIA, VCAP-CID).

VCAP-CIA VCAP Cloud Infrastructure Administrator. This certification demonstrates significant vCloud Director administration experience. Requirements include understanding advanced cloud concepts (including public/private/hybrid clouds, multitenancy, and cloud security); an ability to manage vSphere resources, vCloud Director resources, complex vCloud networks, security, catalogs, and vApps; and the ability to troubleshoot a vCloud Director installation. Individuals must have VCP-Cloud or VCP-Datacenter Virtualization certification first.

VCAP-CID VCAP Cloud Infrastructure Designer. This certification demonstrates the ability to devise a conceptual framework based on business requirements, organize its elements into distinct components, and design a cloud infrastructure that meets the requirements. Requirements include the ability to define goals for the architecture, analyze elements of the framework, and make design decisions that ensure the proper physical and virtual components in the design. Individuals must have VCP-Cloud or VCP-Datacenter Virtualization certification first.

VCAP-DCA   VMware Certified Datacenter Administrator. This certification is for IT administrators, consultants, and technical support engineers who can demonstrate their skills in installing, operating, and managing VMware vSphere technologies for a data center.

VCAP-DCD   VMware Certified Datacenter Designer. This certification is for IT architects who are capable of designing VMware solutions for large, multisite enterprise architectures.

VCAP-DTA   VCAP Desktop Administrator. This certification is for IT administrators, consultants, and technical support engineers who can demonstrate their skills in installing, operating, and managing VMware View technologies for a data center.

VCAP-DTD   VCAP Desktop Designer. This certification is for IT architects who are capable of designing VMware View solutions with ThinApp applications.

VCDX   VMware Certified Design Expert. This is the expert-level category in the VMware certification path. VCDX certifications exist in the areas of data center virtualization (VCDX and VCDX-DCV), desktop (VCDX-DT), and cloud (VCDX-Cloud).

VCDX Blueprint   A description of all the skill areas expected of a VCDX-certified individual. A different blueprint exists for each VCDX certification (VCDX-DCV, VCDX-DT, VCDX-Cloud).

VCDX Boot Camp   A workshop designed for study sessions for individuals pursuing the VCDX certification. The boot camp specializes in the design used and the Panel Defense, to prepare a candidate for the final phase of the VCDX certification process.

VCDX Mock Defense   A 75-minute simulation of a real VCDX Panel Defense. This mock defense can be done in parallel with the VCDX Boot Camp to prepare a candidate for the defense. The mock defense follows the same timeline and content of a real defense.

VCDX-Cloud   VMware Certified Design Expert in Cloud. This is an expert-level certification for architects specializing in cloud solutions. Prerequisites include VCP-DCV, VCP-Cloud, VCAP-CIA, and VCAP-CID.

VCDX-DT   VMware Certified Design Expert in Desktop. This is an expert-level certification for architects specializing in desktop solutions. Prerequisites include VCP-DCV, VCP-DT, VCAP-DTA, and VCAP-DTD.

VCDX-DCV   VMware Certified Design Expert in Datacenter Virtualization. This is an expert-level certification for architects specializing in data center virtualization solutions. Prerequisites include VCP-DCV, VCAP-DCA, and VCAP-DCD.

VCP   VMware Certified Professional. This is the professional-level category in the VMware certification path. VCP certifications exist for the areas of data center virtualization (VCP-DCV), desktop (VCP-DT), and cloud (VCP-Cloud).

VCP-Cloud   VMware Certified Professional in Cloud. This is the professional-level category in the VMware certification path for cloud.

VCP-DT   VMware Certified Professional in Desktop. This is the professional-level category in the VMware certification path for desktop.

VCP-DCV   VMware Certified Professional in Datacenter Virtualization. This is the professional-level category in the VMware certification path for data center virtualization.

Index

A

advanced professional certifications, pathways to VCDX, 5
analyzing
    existing information, 85-86, 91-95, 100
    requirements for troubleshooting scenario, 83
application
    participation as an architect, 18-19
    submitting, 16-17
        fictional components, 18
        mandatory documentation, 19-20
applications, localization, 39
architect, participation as, 18-19
Architecture phase of customer-specific architecture, 32
Arrasjid, John, 2
articulating rationale for design choices, 73, 76
asking panelists questions, 87
asking questions, 82
assumptions, resolving conflicts, 35
availability requirements, including in submitted design, 37

B

benefits of VCDX certification, 11
best practices, 31, 39, 54
blueprint, reviewing, 4
boot camps, running, 22
business goals, understanding
    in cloud-based Design, 71
    in design scenarios, 68

C

candidates, validating, 2
categorizing design requirements and constraints, 33
certification
    VCAP-DCD, 2
    VCDX
        VCDX-Cloud certification track, 8-9
        VCDX-DT certification track, 7-8
        VCDX-DCV certification track, 7
        VCDX-DCV path, 3-4
        workflow, 9
    VMware
        levels of, 3
        solution tracks, 3

checklists
  design defense preparation checklists,
      56-57
  design selection and content, 40
  mock defense, 25
clarifying
  information gaps
    in cloud-based Design, 73
    in design scenarios, 69
  questionable details for troubleshooting,
      92-93, 96-97, 100-101
cloud-based Design Scenario, 70-76
cloud track, prerequisites, 8-9
complexity of submitted designs, 9, 27
conceptual model, including in submitted
    design, 36
conflicts, resolving, 83
  with assumptions, 35
  with constraints, 34
  with requirements, 34
connectivity
  path thrashing, 87-89
  troubleshooting, 88
constraints
  categorizing, 33
  for cloud-based design scenarios, 71-73
  conflicts, resolving, 34
  for design scenarios, 64, 68-69
core components of submitted designs, 30
customer requirements, resolving conflicts,
    34
customer-specific architecture, developing,
    32

D

Dalgleish, Aidan, 35
Damoser, Richard, 2
datacenter virtualization track,
    prerequisites, 7
design defense, 49. *See also* design scenarios
  environment, 46
  familiarity with your design, importance
      of, 54
  interview process, 43

  overview presentation, 50, 58
    example slides, 51-53
    guidelines, 51
    reference material, 53
  Panel Defense, 45
  panelists
    expectations of, 47
    qualifications of, 47
  practicing, 55
  preparation checklists, 56-57
  preparing for, 44
  rules for, 49-50
  strategy for presenting, 54-55
  time management, 44-45
  time requirements, 50
  timeline, 24
design scenarios
  articulating rationale for design choices,
      73, 76
  cloud-based, 70-71
    business goals, 71
    constraints, 71-73
    information gaps, clarifying, 73
    requirements, 71-73
    solutions, validating, 75
    use cases, 71
  desktop-based, 77
  example design scenarios, 62, 66
    business goals, 68
    constraints, 64, 68-69
    requirements, 64, 68-69
    solving, 66
    whiteboarding, 65
  information gaps, clarifying, 69
  panelists, 61-62
  showcasing your skills, 59
  solutions, validating, 70
  time management, 61
  whiteboarding, 61, 69
desktop-based design scenario, 77
desktop virtualization track, prerequisites,
    7-8
developing customer-specific architecture,
    32
development of VCDX certification, 2
development team, 1
diagramming solutions, 69

disaster recovery requirements, including in submitted designs, 37
documentation
    conceptual model, 36
    length recommendations, 35
    reference material, including, 34
    submitted designs, 30

E

English as required language for applications, 39
environment of panel defense, 46
Epping, Duncan, 2-3
exam
    application process, 16-17
        fictional component submission, 18
        mandatory documentation, 19-20
        participation as an architect, 18-19
    design defense
        familiarity with your design, 54
        overview, 58
        overview presentation, 50-53
        practicing, 55
        preparation checklists, 56-57
        strategy for presenting, 54-55
        time requirements, 50
    mock defense, checklist, 25
    preparing for, 21
        VCDX study groups, 21
        with experience, 14-16
    room layout, 23
example design scenarios, 62, 66
    business goals and use cases, 68
    cloud-based, 70
        business goals, 71
        constraints, 71-73
        information gaps, 73
        requirements, 71-73
        solutions, validating, 75
        use cases, 71
    constraints, 64, 68-69
    desktop-based, 77
    information gaps, clarifying, 69
    requirements, 64, 68-69
    solutions, validating, 70

    solving methodically, 66
    whiteboarding, 65, 69
example presentation slides for design defense overview, 51-53
example troubleshooting scenarios, 84, 89
    existing information, analyzing, 85-86, 91-95, 100
    questionable details, clarifying, 96-97, 100-101
    solving methodically, 86-89, 93, 98, 101
    whiteboarding, 86
existing information, analyzing, 85-86, 91-95, 100
expectations of panelists, 47
experience as exam preparation, 14-16
expertise
    demonstrating, 14
    lack of, 15

F

failure of panel defense, notification of, 48
familiarity with your design, importance of, 54
fictional components of submission, 18
file system misalignments, 98

G-H

guidelines for design defense overview presentation, 51

Hald, Andrew, 2
Holmes, Wade, 11, 14
hybrid approach to logical design, 38-39

I

impact of design decisions on other areas, 39
information gaps, clarifying
    in cloud-based Design, 73
    in design scenarios, 69
interview process for design defense, 43

J-K

justifying best practices in submitted designs, 31, 39

KB (Knowledgebase) articles as resource during exam, 98
Khalil, Mostafa, 2
Konuk, Enis, 2

L

lack of expertise, demonstrating, 15
levels of VMware certification, 3
localization, ease of, 1
logical design
    hybrid approach, 38-39
    including in submitted design, 36

M

Manage phase of customer-specific architecture development, 32
manageability requirements, including in submitted design, 37
managing your time, 5
mandatory documentation for application, 19-20
methodical approach to solving design scenarios, 66
methodical troubleshooting approach
    example, 86-89, 93
    troubleshooting, 98, 101
mock defense, 22, 25, 44
models
    conceptual model, 36
    relationship models, 37

N-O

notification of panel defense results, 47

overview presentation for design defense, 50, 58
    example slides, 51-53
    guidelines, 51
    reference, 53

P

panel defense, 45-48
panelists
    asking questions, 82, 87
    of first VCDX exam, 2
    restrictions, 22
    review of submitted designs, 30
    role of in design scenario, 61-62
    viewing as customers, 61
participants of panel defense, 45
passing of panel defense, notification of, 48
path thrashing, 87-89
pathways to VCDX certification, 5
peer review of design defense, 55
performance requirements, including in submitted design, 37
phases of customer-specific architecture development, 32
physical design
    hybrid approach, 38-39
    including in submitted design, 36
Plan phase of customer-specific architecture development, 32
practicing design defense, 55
preparing
    for design defense, 44, 56-57
    for exam, 21
        experience, 14-16
        review process, 25-26
prerequisites
    for cloud track, 8-9
    for datacenter virtualization track, 7
    for desktop virtualization track, 7-8
    for VCP-level certification, 5
professional-level certifications, pathways to VCDX, 5
proposed solutions, validating, 70, 75
psychometrics, 1

Q

qualifications of panelists, 47
questionable details, clarifying, 92-93,
     96-97, 100-101
questions, asking panelists, 82

R

Rajani, Mahesh, 2
rationale for design choices, articulating,
     73, 76
recoverability requirements, including in
     submitted design, 37
reference material
     for design defense overview, 53
     including in documentation, 34
registration fees, 17
relationship models, 37
required documentation for application,
     19-20
requirements
     analyzing for troubleshooting scenario,
          83
     categorizing, 33
     complexity in submitted designs, 27
     conflicts, resolving, 34
     for cloud-based design scenarios, 71-73
     for design scenarios, 64, 68-69
resolving conflicts, 83
     with assumptions, 35
     with constraints, 34
     with requirements, 34
restrictions on panelist participation, 22
reviewing
     for exam, 25-26
     test blueprint, 4
Risinger, Craig, 2
role of panelists in design scenario, 61-62
room layout for exam, 23
rules for design defense, 49-50
running a boot camp, 22

S

sections in VCDX Design Defense
     Blueprint, 28
security requirements, including in
     submitted design, 37
showcasing your skills, 59
SLAs (Service Level Agreements), 34
slides
     for design defense overview presentation,
          50-53
     reference material for overview
          presentation, 53
solution tracks, VMware certification, 3
solutions
     required complexity in, 27
     validating in design scenarios, 70, 75
solving troubleshooting scenarios
     methodically, 98, 101
strategy for presenting your design defense,
     54-55
study groups, 21
submitted designs
     core components, 30
     justifying best practices, 39
     length recommendations, 35
     panelist review of, 30
     requirements and, 33
submitting your application, 16-17
     fictional components, 18
     mandatory documentation, 19-20

T

test plans, 31
thinking aloud, 82
time management, 5
     for design defense, 44-45, 50
     in design scenario, 61
timeline for running the defense, 24
traceability, categorizing design
     requirements, 33
Transition phases of customer-specific
     architecture, 32

troubleshooting scenarios, 81
  ask questions, 82
  conflicting information, 83
  example scenarios, 84-89
    existing, 85-86, 91-93
    solving, 86-89, 93
    whiteboarding, 86
  example troubleshooting, 93-101
  requirements analysis, 83
  thinking aloud, 82
  whiteboarding, 82
Tuite, Melissa, 2

U-V

use cases, understanding in design
    scenarios, 68, 71

validating candidates, 2
  in cloud-based design, 75
  in design scenario, 70
VCA (VMware Certified Associate)
    certification, 3
VCAP (VMware Certified Advanced
    Professional), 3-4
VCAP-DCA (Datacenter Administrator)
    certification, 4

VCAP-DCD (Datacenter Design)
    certification, 2-4
VCDX (VMware Certified Design Expert)
    certification, 3-5
VCDX-Cloud certification track, 8-9
VCDX Design Defense Blueprint, sections,
    28
VCDX-DT certification track, 7-8
VCDX-DCV certification path, 3-4, 7
VCP (VMware Certified Professional)
    certification, 1
viewing panelists as customers, 61
Vision phase of customer-specific
    architecture development, 32
VMware certification, 3
VMWare Knowledgebase articles as
    resource during exam, 98
VXLAN (Virtual eXtensible LAN), 73

W-X-Y-Z

Wanguhu, Kamau, 2
whiteboarding, 82
  for design scenarios, 61, 65, 69
  example troubleshooting scenario, 86
workflow of VCDX certification, 9

We Want to Hear from You!

As the reader of this book, *you* are our most important critic and commentator. We value your opinion and want to know what we're doing right, what we could do better, what areas you'd like to see us publish in, and any other words of wisdom you're willing to pass our way.

As an associate publisher for Pearson, I welcome your comments. You can e-mail or write me directly to let me know what you did or didn't like about this book— as well as what we can do to make our books better.

Please note that I cannot help you with technical problems related to the topic of this book. We do have a User Services group, however, where I will forward specific technical questions related to the book.

When you write, please be sure to include this book's title and author, as well as your name, e-mail address, and phone number. I will carefully review your comments and share them with the author and editors who worked on the book.

E-mail: VMwarePress@vmware.com

Mail: David Dusthimer
        Associate Publisher
        Pearson
        800 East 96th Street
        Indianapolis, IN 46240 USA

Reader Services

Visit our website and register this book for convenient access to any updates, downloads, or errata that might be available for this book.